26

STUDY GUIDE

Elizabethan England, c1568–1603

AQA - GCSE

Published by Clever Lili Limited.

contact@cleverlili.com

First published 2020

ISBN 978-1-913887-25-4

Copyright notice

All rights reserved. No part of this publication may be reproduced in any form or by any means (including photocopying or storing it in any medium by electronic means and whether or not transiently or incidentally to some other use of this publication) with the written permission of the copyright owner. Applications for the copyright owner's written permission should be addressed to the publisher.

Clever Lili has made every effort to contact copyright holders for permission for the use of copyright material. We will be happy, upon notification, to rectify any errors or omissions and include any appropriate rectifications in future editions.

Cover by: Everett Collection on Shutterstock

Icons by: flaticon and freepik

Contributors: Hayleigh Snow, Emily Bishop, Muirin Gillespie-Gallery, Jordan Hobbis, Donna Garvey

Edited by Paul Connolly and Rebecca Parsley

Design by Evgeni Veskov and Will Fox

All rights reserved

DISCOVER MORE OF OUR GCSE HISTORY STUDY GUIDES
GCSEHistory.com and Clever Lili

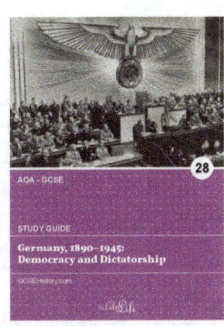
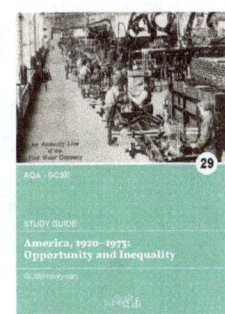

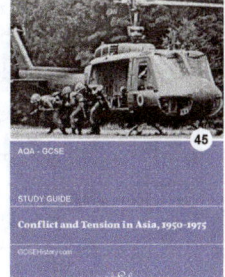

THE GUIDES ARE EVEN BETTER WITH OUR GCSE/IGCSE HISTORY WEBSITE APP AND MOBILE APP

GCSE History is a text and voice web and mobile app that allows you to easily revise for your GCSE/IGCSE exams wherever you are - it's like having your own personal GCSE history tutor. Whether you're at home or on the bus, GCSE History provides you with thousands of convenient bite-sized facts to help you pass your exams with flying colours. We cover all topics - with more than 120,000 questions - across the Edexcel, AQA and CIE exam boards.

Contents

- How to use this book 5
- What is this book about? 6
- Revision suggestions 8

Timelines
- Elizabethan England, c1568-1603 12

Elizabeth's Court and Government
- Elizabeth's Background 14
- Elizabethan Government 16
- The Threat from France 18
- The Treaty of Cateau-Cambrésis 19
- Elizabeth and Marriage 19
- The Essex Rebellion 21
- Elizabeth's Problems in the 1590s 22

Life in Elizabethan Times
- Elizabethan Society 23
- A 'Golden Age' 24
- Elizabethan Theatre 25
- The Globe - Historic Environment 26
- Elizabethan Architecture 27
- Hardwick Hall - Historic Environment 28
- Kenilworth Castle - Robert Dudley 29
- Kenilworth Castle - Historic Environment 30
- Elizabethan Leisure 32
- Elizabethan Education 32
- Poverty in Elizabethan England 33
- Paupers and Poverty 34
- Response to the Poor 35
- Poor Laws 36
- Drake - Discoveries 37
- Hawkins - Discoveries 38
- Raleigh - Discoveries 39
- Navigation and Exploration 40

Troubles at Home and Abroad
- Henry VIII and the Reformation 41
- Edward VI and the Reformation 42
- Mary I and the Reformation 43
- The Religious Settlement 43
- Arrival of Mary, Queen of Scots 45
- The Northern Rebellion 46
- The Papal Bull 47
- Ridolfi 48
- Throckmorton 48
- Babington 49
- Counter Reformation - Catholic Threat 50
- Puritan Threat 51
- Presbyterians - Puritan Threat 52
- Response to the Puritan Threat 52
- Mary Queen of Scots' Trial 53
- Deterioration in Relations with Spain 54
- Poor Relations with Spain - the Role of King Philip II 54
- Poor Relations with Spain - the Role of the Duke of Anjou 55
- Poor Relations with Spain - the Role of the Nonsuch Treaty 56
- Poor Relations with Spain - the Role of Robert Dudley 56
- Poor Relations with Spain - the Role of the English Privateers 57
- Cadiz - Naval Warfare 57
- Tactics and Technology - Naval Warfare 58
- The Spanish Armada 59
- The Armada and Propaganda 60

- Glossary 61
- Index 65

HOW TO USE THIS BOOK

In this study guide, you will see a series of icons, highlighted words and page references. The key below will help you quickly establish what these mean and where to go for more information.

Icons

WHAT questions cover the key events and themes.

WHO questions cover the key people involved.

WHEN questions cover the timings of key events.

WHERE questions cover the locations of key moments.

WHY questions cover the reasons behind key events.

HOW questions take a closer look at the way in which events, situations and trends occur.

IMPORTANCE questions take a closer look at the significance of events, situations, and recurrent trends and themes.

DECISIONS questions take a closer look at choices made at events and situations during this era.

Highlighted words

Abdicate - occasionally, you will see certain words highlighted within an answer. This means that, if you need it, you'll find an explanation of the word or phrase in the glossary which starts on **page 61**.

Page references

Tudor *(p.7)* - occasionally, a certain subject within an answer is covered in more depth on a different page. If you'd like to learn more about it, you can go directly to the page indicated.

WHAT IS THIS BOOK ABOUT?

Elizabethan England 1586-1603 is split into 4 key enquiries: Elizabeth's court and Parliament, life in Elizabethan times, roubles abroad and at home, and the historic environment.

Purpose
This study will help you understand the complexities and challenges Elizabeth I faced during her rule. You will investigate themes such as power, law and order, government, religion, and economy and society. This course will enable you to develop the historical skills of causation and consequence, and encourage you to question critical sources.

Enquiries
Elizabethan England 1586-1603 is split into 4 key enquiries. Elizabeth's court and Parliament, life in Elizabethan times, troubles at home and abroad, and the historic environment.

- Enquiry 1 looks at the Elizabethan court and Parliament. You will also study Elizabeth's background, the problems she faced when she came to power, and how she resolved them.
- Enquiry 2 looks at life in Elizabethan times. You will investigate the extent to which this period could be considered a 'golden age', and also look into the age of exploration and discoveries.
- Enquiry 3 looks at troubles at home and abroad. You will study the religious challenges to Elizabeth's rule from the Catholics within the country as well as the threat posed by her cousin, Mary, Queen of Scots.
- Enquiry 4 looks at the historic environment. The site chosen changes each year and you must investigate how the site and historical developments in this period link together.

Key Individuals
Some of the key individuals studied on this course include:

- Queen Elizabeth I.
- King Philip II.
- Mary, Queen of Scots.
- Pope Pius V.
- Robert Dudley.
- Robert Devereux.
- Sir Francis Walsingham.
- William Cecil.
- Sir Francis Drake.
- John Hawkins.
- Sir Walter Raleigh.

Key Events
Some of the key events you will study on this course include:

- The Religious Settlement.
- The Northern Rebellion.
- The Ridolfi Plot.
- The Throckmorton Plot.
- The Babington Plot.
- The Execution of Mary, Queen of Scots.
- The Essex Rebellion.

Assessment
Elizabethan England 1586-1603 forms part of paper 2 which you have a total of 2 hours to complete. You should spend 1 hour on this section of the paper. There will be 4 questions which will assess what you have learnt on the Elizabethan England 1586-1603 course.

- Question 1 is worth 8 marks. This question requires you to examine an interpretation and assesses your ability to analyse and evaluate how convincing it is using your contextual knowledge to challenge or corroborate what is being said.

WHAT IS THIS BOOK ABOUT?

- Question 2 is worth 8 marks. This question requires you to explain the importance of a different theme or event by using your contextual knowledge and looking at the consequences.
- Question 3 is worth 8 marks. This question requires you to show your knowledge and understanding of the key features and characteristics of the course. You will have the opportunity to demonstrate your ability to explain and analyse historical events using 2nd order concepts such as causation, consequence, change, continuity, similarity and difference.
- Question 4 is worth 16 marks. Similar skills to those needed in question 3 are assessed, but you are also required to make a judgement in an extended response through an investigation of your historic environment.

REVISION SUGGESTIONS

Revision! A dreaded word. Everyone knows it's coming, everyone knows how much it helps with your exam performance, and everyone struggles to get started! We know you want to do the best you can in your GCSEs, but schools aren't always clear on the best way to revise. This can leave students wondering:

- ✓ How should I plan my revision time?
- ✓ How can I beat procrastination?
- ✓ What methods should I use? Flash cards? Re-reading my notes? Highlighting?

Luckily, you no longer need to guess at the answers. Education researchers have looked at all the available revision studies, and the jury is in. They've come up with some key pointers on the best ways to revise, as well as some thoughts on popular revision methods that aren't so helpful. The next few pages will help you understand what we know about the best revision methods.

How can I beat procrastination?

This is an age-old question, and it applies to adults as well! Have a look at our top three tips below.

◎ Reward yourself

When we think a task we have to do is going to be boring, hard or uncomfortable, we often put if off and do something more 'fun' instead. But we often don't really enjoy the 'fun' activity because we feel guilty about avoiding what we should be doing. Instead, get your work done and promise yourself a reward after you complete it. Whatever treat you choose will seem all the sweeter, and you'll feel proud for doing something you found difficult. Just do it!

◎ Just do it!

We tend to procrastinate when we think the task we have to do is going to be difficult or dull. The funny thing is, the most uncomfortable part is usually making ourselves sit down and start it in the first place. Once you begin, it's usually not nearly as bad as you anticipated.

◎ Pomodoro technique

The pomodoro technique helps you trick your brain by telling it you only have to focus for a short time. Set a timer for 20 minutes and focus that whole period on your revision. Turn off your phone, clear your desk, and work. At the end of the 20 minutes, you get to take a break for five. Then, do another 20 minutes. You'll usually find your rhythm and it becomes easier to carry on because it's only for a short, defined chunk of time.

Spaced practice

We tend to arrange our revision into big blocks. For example, you might tell yourself: "This week I'll do all my revision for the Cold War, then next week I'll do the Medicine Through Time unit."

REVISION SUGGESTIONS

This is called **massed practice**, because all revision for a single topic is done as one big mass.

But there's a better way! Try **spaced practice** instead. Instead of putting all revision sessions for one topic into a single block, space them out. See the example below for how it works.

This means planning ahead, rather than leaving revision to the last minute - but the evidence strongly suggests it's worth it. You'll remember much more from your revision if you use **spaced practice** rather than organising it into big blocks. Whichever method you choose, though, remember to reward yourself with breaks.

Spaced practice (more effective):

week 1	week 2	week 3	week 4
Topic 1	Topic 1	Topic 1	Topic 1
Topic 2	Topic 2	Topic 2	Topic 2
Topic 3	Topic 3	Topic 3	Topic 3
Topic 4	Topic 4	Topic 4	Topic 4

Massed practice (less effective)

week 1	week 2	week 3	week 4
Topic 1	Topic 2	Topic 3	Topic 4

REVISION SUGGESTIONS

 What methods should I use to revise?

Self-testing/flash cards

Self explanation/mind-mapping

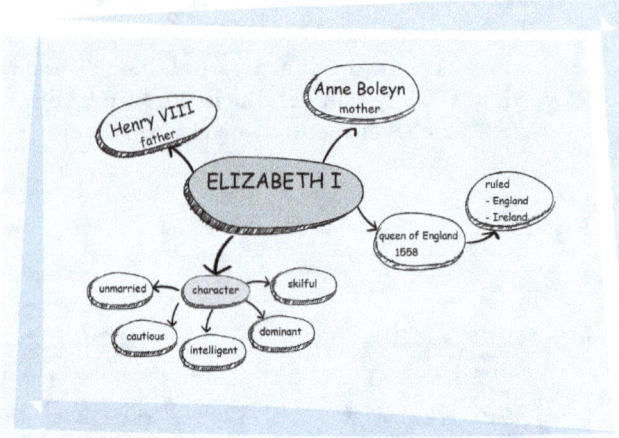

The research shows a clear winner for revision methods - **self-testing**. A good way to do this is with flash cards. Flash cards are really useful for helping you recall short – but important – pieces of information, like names and dates.

Side A - question

Side B - answer

Write questions on one side of the cards, and the answers on the back. This makes answering the questions and then testing yourself easy. Put all the cards you get right in a pile to one side, and only repeat the test with the ones you got wrong - this will force you to work on your weaker areas.

pile with right answers

pile with wrong answers

As this book has a quiz question structure itself, you can use it for this technique.

Another good revision method is **self-explanation**. This is where you explain how and why one piece of information from your course linked with another piece.

 This can be done with mind-maps, where you draw the links and then write explanations for how they connect. For example, President Truman is connected with anti-communism because of the Truman Doctrine.

REVISION SUGGESTIONS

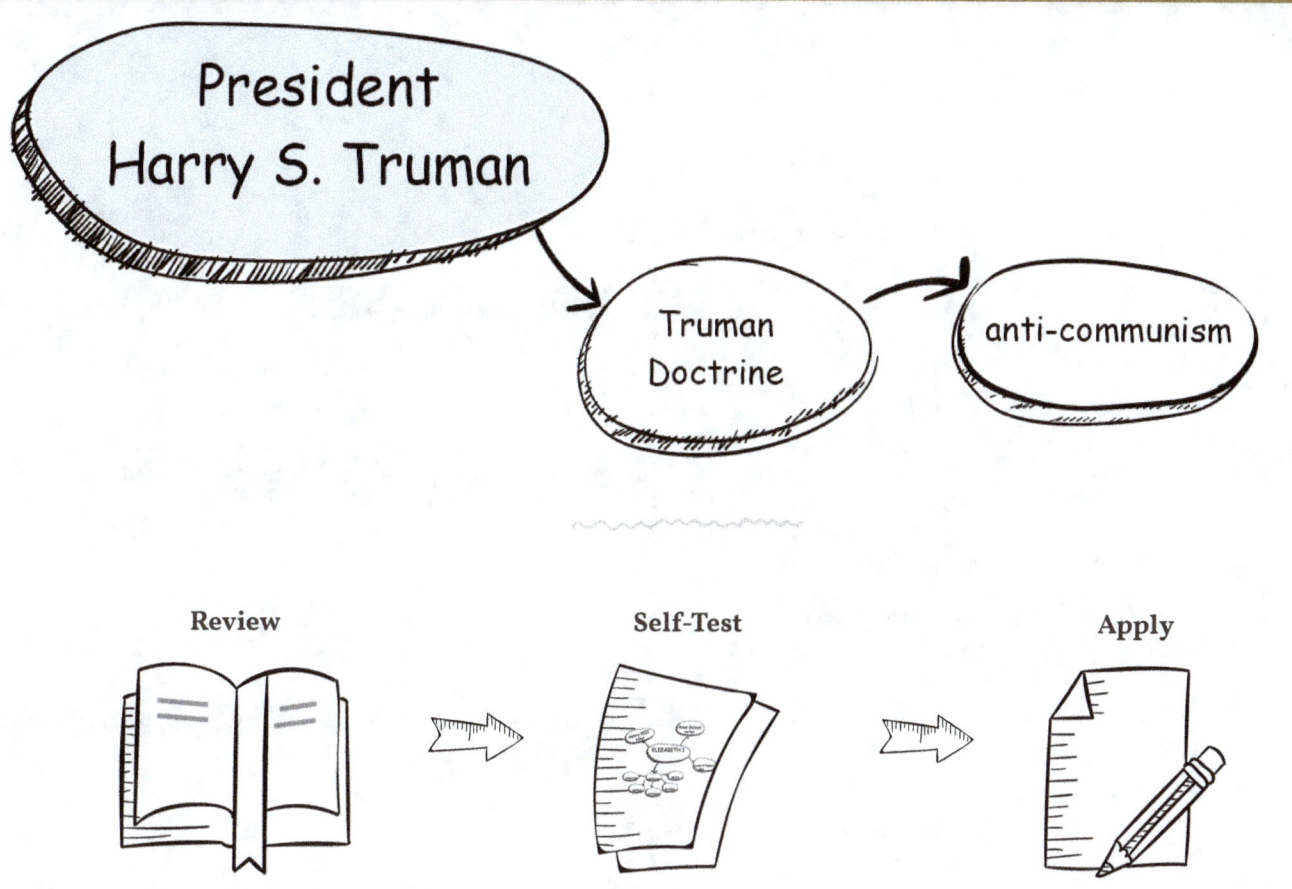

Start by highlighting or re-reading to create your flashcards for self-testing.

Test yourself with flash cards. Make mind maps to explain the concepts.

Apply your knowledge on practice exam questions.

Which revision techniques should I be cautious about?

Highlighting and **re-reading** are not necessarily bad strategies - but the research does say they're less effective than flash cards and mind-maps.

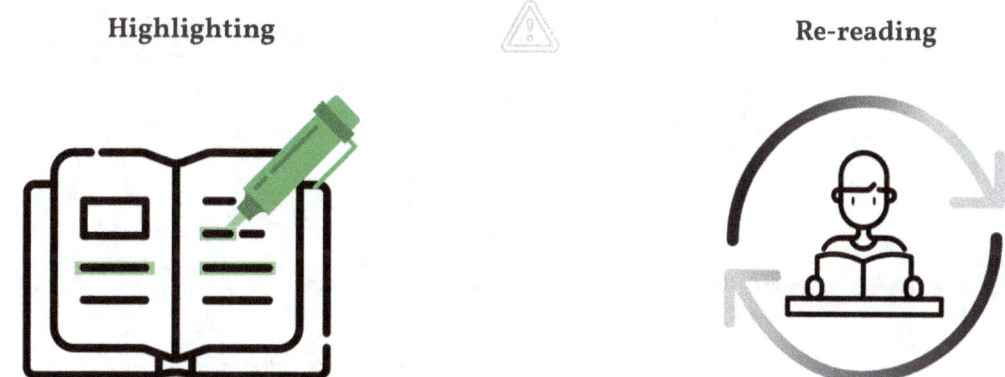

If you do use these methods, make sure they are **the first step to creating flash cards**. Really engage with the material as you go, rather than switching to autopilot.

ELIZABETHAN ENGLAND, C1568-1603

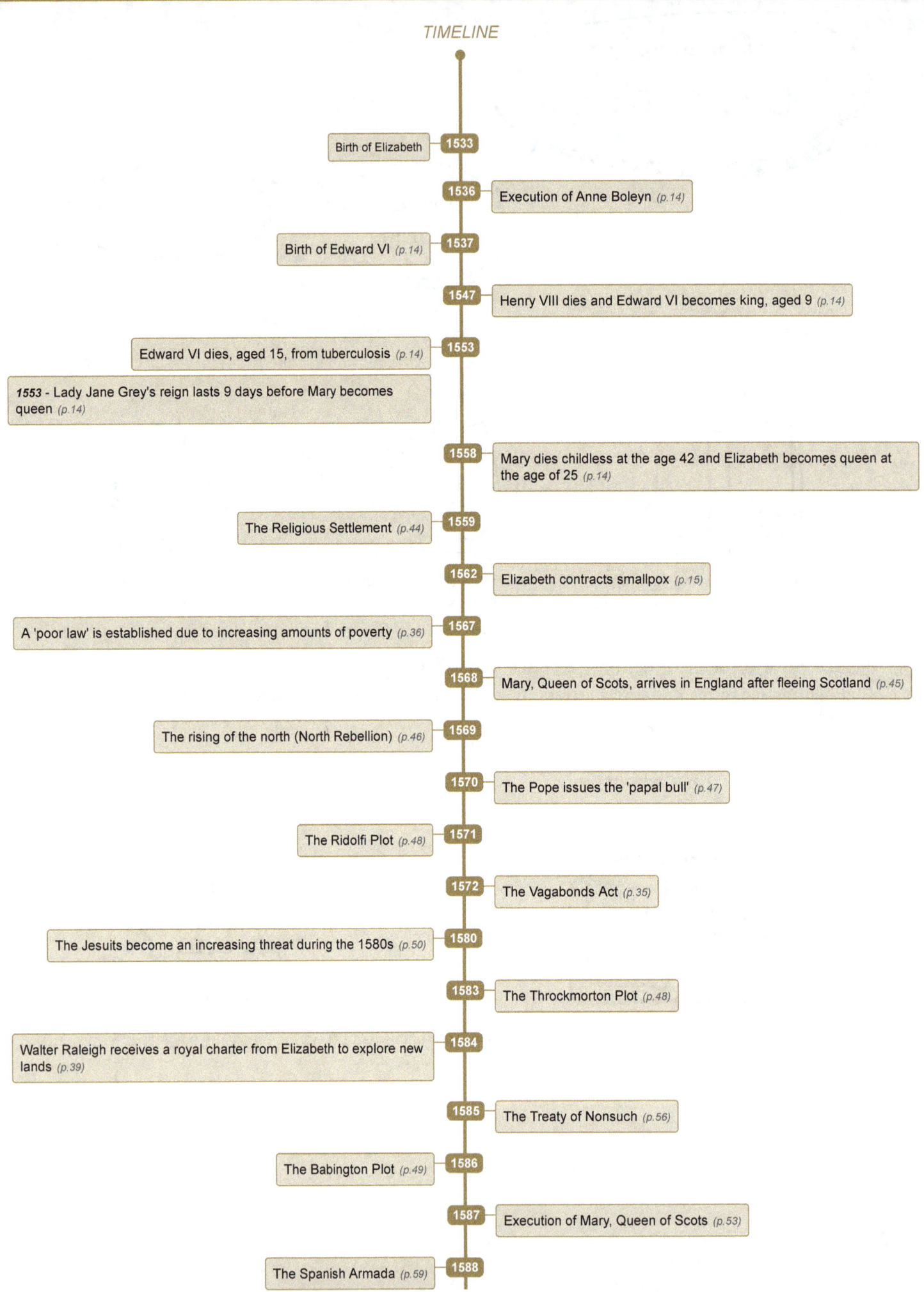

ELIZABETHAN ENGLAND, C1568-1603

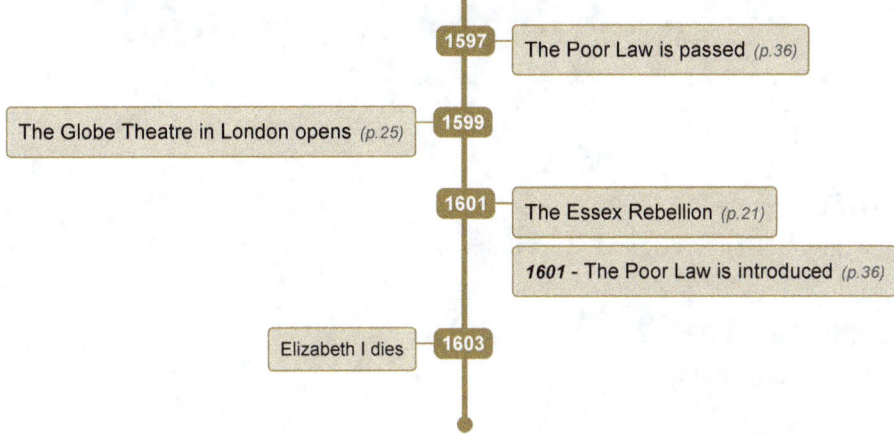

- 1597 — The Poor Law is passed *(p.36)*
- 1599 — The Globe Theatre in London opens *(p.25)*
- 1601 — The Essex Rebellion *(p.21)*
- *1601* - The Poor Law is introduced *(p.36)*
- 1603 — Elizabeth I dies

ELIZABETH'S BACKGROUND

Elizabeth's childhood was not as simple as we may assume. Some distressing experiences shaped the queen she would later become.

Who was Elizabeth I?
Elizabeth was the daughter of Henry VIII and Anne Boleyn.

Which house was Elizabeth I from?
Elizabeth was from the House of Tudor.

How old was Elizabeth I when she ascended to the throne?
Elizabeth was 25 years old when she became queen.

When did Elizabeth I become queen?
She ruled England and Ireland from 1558, after the death of her sister, Mary I, and reigned until her own death in 1603.

Who were Elizabeth I's siblings?
Elizabeth I had two half-siblings, Edward VI and Mary I.

Who was Elizabeth I's predecessor?
Mary I, Elizabeth's half-sister, was Queen of England before Elizabeth I.

How experienced was Elizabeth I when she became queen in 1558?
Elizabeth I was young and inexperienced when she became Queen of England in 1558.

What type of leader was Elizabeth I?
Queen Elizabeth I was a strong-minded leader. She ruled England during a time of challenges at home and abroad.

What were Elizabeth I's strengths?
Elizabeth had several important character traits which were her strengths.
- She was independent. This meant she could have her choice of suitors rather than be controlled by a foreign husband.
- She was cautious. She understood the balance needed to maintain her reign, particularly regarding the rivalry between Protestants and Catholics.
- She was an intelligent and well-educated queen. She spoke foreign languages, enjoyed theatre *(p.25)* and music, and shrewdly rewarded loyalty to those who served her.
- She was dominant. She was always ready to assert her power and refused to be controlled by anyone.
- She was a skilful self-publicist. She worked hard to create the right image and ensured her propaganda presented her well.

How did trauma shape Elizabeth I's character?
Elizabeth had a traumatic childhood that shaped her character as queen.
- Elizabeth's father, Henry VIII, divorced her mother, Anne Boleyn, accusing her of adultery. Boleyn was eventually executed.
- Henry VIII married *(p.19)* his third wife, Jane Seymour, only 11 days after Anne Boleyn was executed.

- Elizabeth was estranged from her father, Henry VIII for some of her childhood.
- When Elizabeth's half-sister, Mary, became queen she imprisoned Elizabeth in the Tower of London and accused her of supporting a rebellion against her.

What problems did Elizabeth I inherit when she came to the throne in 1558?

Elizabeth faced a number of problems in 1558.

- She was left with debts of £300,000 by Mary I, following an expensive war with France.
- She was female and some people feared England would be seen as a weak country because most others at the time, such as Spain, were ruled by men.
- Elizabeth had been declared illegitimate following her mother's execution. Many saw her as an illegitimate daughter from an unlawful marriage (p.19), and not the rightful Queen of England.
- Religion was a huge problem. The country had switched from Catholicism to Protestantism and then back again since Henry VIII's death in 1547. It was a religious rollercoaster, causing conflict and confusion.
- There were threats from Catholics. Many were opposed to Elizabeth's Religious Settlement (p.43) and wanted her Catholic cousin, Mary, Queen of Scots (p.45), on the throne.
- The government needed more money but Elizabeth inherited a country riddled with poverty (p.33). Increased taxation would be an unpopular and dangerous move.

Why was Elizabeth I's legitimacy questioned?

Catholics considered Elizabeth was born out of wedlock as the Catholic church did not recognise Henry VIII's divorce from Catherine of Aragon. In their eyes, he was still married (p.19) to his first wife, which meant Elizabeth must be illegitimate.

Why was gender an issue for Elizabeth I in 1558?

Most people wanted a man as the monarch and women did not have much influence in society. When England was previously ruled by a female - Mary I - her reign was short and unsuccessful, partly because the country lost a war and incurred huge debt in the process.

Why was marriage an issue for Elizabeth I in 1558?

Marriage (p.19) was a problem for Elizabeth. As a queen in the 16th century, she was expected to marry and have children. However, during this time men had more authority than women. Elizabeth did not want to submit to the authority of a husband. Although she had many suitors, she never married.

What was Elizabeth I known as?

Elizabeth never married (p.19) and was later known as 'The Virgin Queen'.

Why was succession important during the reign of Elizabeth I?

There were fears over the succession as Elizabeth had not produced an heir who could take the throne after her. This caused fear and uncertainty about the future, accentuated in 1562 when Elizabeth nearly died from smallpox.

What was the threat to Elizabeth I from France in 1558?

England had been at war with France intermittently since 1522 and it had been costly. When Elizabeth came to the throne in 1558, she inherited a £300,000 debt from Henry VIII and Mary I. She needed to find a solution to this hole in the country's finances.

What were the financial challenges Elizabeth I had to face?

As well as inheriting a considerable debt, Elizabeth needed to reduce government spending. She did this by reducing her own household spending and selling off land belonging to the Crown. This took 20 years, but by 1585 she had paid off the debt and built a surplus of £300,000.

How was the country financed during Elizabeth I's rule?

As monarch, Elizabeth was expected to fund the costs of running the country. She had to raise money from taxes, legislation which needed the support and approval of Parliament.

 How did Elizabeth I gain support in the country?

Elizabeth used 5 main strategies to gain the support of her court and the nobles in Parliament.

- ☑ Elizabeth bought the loyalty of her court and nobles using patronage. She granted 'leases in reversion' to loyal nobles. These were effectively a grant of freedom and money from the queen.
- ☑ Elizabeth could reward courtiers with titles, power, and positions of authority without it costing the treasury any money. She gave nobles social status and power, conditional on them supporting her as the queen. She made sure to offer minor nobles social status, too, to broaden her power base of influence.
- ☑ Elizabeth also granted nobles monopolies over whole industries in order to ensure her power base was stable.
- ☑ Elizabeth would go on visits, known as progresses, with the Royal Court. During these expeditions, the queen would stay at wealthy nobles' houses which was seen as a great privilege for them.
- ☑ Elizabeth worked to shape her public image. Elizabeth commissioned propaganda portraits of herself which included images of power and purity.

DID YOU KNOW?

Elizabeth had a troubled childhood.

She was banished by her father, Henry VIII, and then imprisoned by her sister, Mary I! While in the Tower of London she wrote the famous 'Tide Letter' to Mary, pleading for mercy.

ELIZABETHAN GOVERNMENT

In Elizabethan England, everyone worked to a strict hierarchy. The government was no exception and had many factions who took on key roles in running the country.

 How did the government work under Elizabeth I?

Elizabeth, as monarch, had royal prerogative. This meant only she could make decisions on certain issues, such as succession. However, she did rely on her court, Parliament and Privy Council for some matters.

 Who controlled the Elizabethan government?

The queen had the most power, as she controlled the royal court, Parliament and Privy Council.

 How much control did the queen have over the Elizabethan government?

The queen had control over the following things:

- ☑ She controlled foreign policy.
- ☑ She could dispense lands, money and jobs to people.
- ☑ She could accept or reject parliamentary legislation.

What were key features of the royal court in Elizabethan government?

The royal court and the government were not the same thing. Court was a collection of people, or courtiers.

- The court was the centre of political power and the source for trends and fashion.
- The court was very extravagant and consisted of the highest nobles down to ladies-in-waiting and servants.
- The court would follow Elizabeth wherever she went across the country.
- It held many tournaments, jousts, plays and feasts; success in a tournament could get you noticed by Queen Elizabeth *(p.14)* I. However, banishment from court was considered a disgrace.

How did the queen control her court as part of the Elizabethan government?

Elizabeth used patronage, rewards of monopolies, and the bestowal of favour upon people in order to be able to motivate and control courtiers.

Why was the court important to the Elizabethan government?

Elizabethan court was important in many ways.
- Firstly, court greeted many artists and explorers from around the world, making it centre stage for the English Renaissance.
- Secondly, attendance at court was desirable, so Elizabeth used it to ensure the loyalty of nobles.

What was the Privy Council in Elizabeth I's government?

The Privy Council consisted of 19 men who advised the monarch and met at least three times each week. They had two main functions.
- The Privy Council was responsible for the day-to-day running of the country and its members were Elizabeth's main advisers.
- They also negotiated between Parliament and the Crown. William Cecil did this particularly effectively, and was a strong advocate in Parliament of Elizabeth's policies.

How were the councillors chosen to be part of Elizabeth I's government?

Elizabeth chose her councillors carefully, ensuring they were people she could trust but also retaining previous council members from her predecessors. She was successful in ensuring they worked loyally for her.

Who were the important figures in the Privy Council within the Elizabethan government?

Some important Privy Council members were:
- William Paulet.
- Walter Mildmay.
- Christopher Hatton.
- Philip Sidney.
- Thomas Radclyffe, Earl of Sussex.

What role did Parliament play in Elizabethan government?

Parliament was divided into the House of Lords and the House of Commons, but it had much less power than parliament today. It could pass laws and grant increased taxation, but Elizabeth kept it under tight control and only called it 13 times in her 45-year reign.

What was the Queen's relationship like with Parliament during Elizabethan government?

During her reign, MPs became more assertive and were in conflict with Elizabeth about the following:
- Parliament wanted Elizabeth to marry *(p.19)* and produce an heir to secure the line of succession.
- Some Puritan MPs disagreed with the Religious Settlement *(p.43)* and threatened not to grant her taxes.
- Peter Wentworth argued that MPs did not have freedom of speech. As a result, he was sent to the Tower of London for a month.

- Some MPs argued that monopolies were unfair and were being abused. In 1597-8 and 1601 they protested against them.

Who were the advisers in Elizabeth I's government?

Elizabeth had three key advisers:

- William Cecil was appointed Secretary of State in 1558. He was her most important minister and guided her for 40 years.
- Robert Dudley was known as the Earl of Leicester and was a trusted adviser until he died in 1588. He and Elizabeth were very close and it was rumoured they were lovers.
- Sir Francis Walsingham was in charge of the secret service and advised on foreign affairs. In 1586, he uncovered the plot that led to the execution of Mary, Queen of Scots *(p.45)*.

What was the role of Lord Lieutenants in the Elizabethan government?

These were appointed by Elizabeth. They collected taxes and settled arguments. They were also responsible for raising armies to fight for the queen. This position could lead to great power and influence.

What was the role of Justices of the Peace in Elizabeth I's government?

Each county had several justices of the peace who kept order. They were selected from the gentry and had to enforce laws. Justices of the peace worked voluntarily but their position held a lot of status.

> **DID YOU KNOW?**
>
> **Elizabeth had considerable control over parliament.**
> When it tried to force marriage on her, she refused and claimed she had married the country. She even wore her coronation ring on her wedding finger!

THE THREAT FROM FRANCE

France was a threat to Elizabeth as soon as she took the throne. Mary I's war against the French was unsuccessful and it was now up to Elizabeth to defend her country.

What was the situation between France and England when Elizabeth became queen?

A war with France had ended in the Siege of Calais in 1558. The French seized Calais, which was England's toehold on mainland Europe.

What happened to Calais at the end of the war with France during the early years of Elizabeth's rule?

The Treaty of Cateau-Cambrésis *(p.19)* recognised Calais as being 'in French custody'.

Why was France a threat during the early years of Elizabeth's rule?

There were two important reasons why France was seen as a threat to England.

- Scotland was run by the Queen Regent, the French Mary of Guise. She invited French soldiers to defend Scotland from England. France was a Catholic country in the 1550s and Elizabeth was an English Protestant.
- Following the marriage *(p.19)* of Mary, Queen of Scots *(p.45)*, to the heir to the French throne, many in France believed she was also the rightful Queen of England.

> **DID YOU KNOW?**
>
> **The Siege of Calais was actually part of the Italian War of 1551–1559.**
>
> France was at war with the Holy Roman Empire and Spain to try and reclaim the whole of France and Italy. Calais was controlled by England at the time and Mary I was married to the king of Spain, which meant England was dragged into the war.

THE TREATY OF CATEAU-CAMBRÉSIS

Both England and Spain agreed to settle their differences with France. This diplomatic agreement would become known as the Treaty of Cateau-Cambrésis.

What was the Treaty of Cateau-Cambrésis?

The Treaty of Cateau-Cambrésis ended the war in 1559 and gave Elizabeth some security. Mary I had been married *(p.19)* to King Philip II of Spain *(p.54)*, who dragged England into war against France. When Elizabeth took the throne she was very anxious for peace.

Why was the Treaty of Cateau-Cambrésis needed?

Mary I was married *(p.19)* to the King of Spain. England joined the war between Spain and France, supporting King Philip II of Spain *(p.54)*.

> **DID YOU KNOW?**
>
> **The Treaty of Cateau-Cambrésis actually consisted of two treaties!**
>
> The first was signed between England and France, and the second between France and Spain.

ELIZABETH AND MARRIAGE

'I have already joyned myself in marriage to an Husband, namely, the Kingdom.' - Elizabeth I, 1559

What was the issue over Elizabeth and marriage?

Elizabeth was 25 when she came to the throne. By Tudor standards, this was old to remain unmarried.

Why was marriage a problem for Elizabeth I?

Elizabeth's unmarried status was a problem as, without a husband, she would not be able to produce a legitimate heir to carry on the Tudor name.

What did Parliament think of the marriage issue for Elizabeth I?
Elizabeth's marital status was often an issue for her Parliament. However, in 1566 she got angry as its members discussed her marriage after she had forbidden them from doing so.

How did smallpox increase people's fear about Elizabeth I not marrying?
In 1562, Elizabeth contracted smallpox and nearly died. This accentuated fears about her not marrying as it highlighted the lack of certainty about the country's future on her death.

Who were Elizabeth I's suitors for marriage?
Elizabeth did have a number of possible suitors.
- Robert Dudley, the Earl of Leicester, was close friends with Elizabeth. The two did not marry as there was suspicion surrounding the death of his first wife.
- King Philip II of Spain (p.54) was previously married to Elizabeth's half-sister and predecessor, Mary I. However, he was Catholic and Protestant Elizabeth was worried about the religious tensions this marriage would cause.
- Francis, Duke of Alencon, was heir to the French throne. However, Francis died in 1584. After this, Elizabeth was destined to be alone.

What were the advantages of Elizabeth I remaining unmarried?
There were six advantages to Elizabeth staying single.
- Elizabeth could keep sole control of the government.
- She had a number of suitors from different countries. Refusal to choose between them made foreign relations easier.
- As there was no successor, she was the focus of all power.
- By not marrying into a foreign power she was able to prevent a rebellion similar to the Wyatt Rebellion in 1554, which happened after Mary I married King Philip of Spain.
- If Elizabeth married an English husband this could cause jealousy between families and rivalries between England's important men. By not marrying, she kept the balance of power intact.
- Giving birth was risky during this time and often resulted in the death of the mother. By not marrying, Elizabeth was not forced to have a child and therefore did not risk death in this way.

What would have been the advantages of Elizabeth I marrying?
There would have been five advantages to Elizabeth marrying.
- There would be no uncertainty over who would inherit the throne.
- People had a secure future so rebellions were less likely.
- The Privy Council was frustrated as it felt Elizabeth being single made the country vulnerable; her marriage would have addressed this.
- If Elizabeth did marry then Mary, Queen of Scots (p.45), would not inherit the throne.
- Marriage to foreign royalty would have made a powerful alliance for England to secure its position.

Why did Elizabeth I decide not to marry?
There were many reasons Elizabeth decided not to marry.
- She could be portrayed as the 'Virgin Queen' who put England before herself.
- It allowed her to remain independent of any foreign influence.
- It prevented the development of factions or jealousy with her courtiers or Privy Council members.

> **DID YOU KNOW?**
>
> **Only one suitor tried to court Elizabeth in person!**
> The Duke of Alençon, who was 22 years younger than Elizabeth, approached her at court before they exchanged letters. She referred to him affectionately as her 'frog'.

THE ESSEX REBELLION

Robert Devereux, 2nd Earl of Essex, tried to gather the people of London to start a rebellion and overthrow the government. He failed and was executed for treason in 1601.

What was the Essex Rebellion?

The Essex Rebellion happened in 1601 during Elizabeth's years of decline. The Earl of Essex, Robert Devereux, wanted to overthrow the government.

What were the causes of the Essex Rebellion?

There were 6 causes of the Essex Rebellion:
- Elizabeth's government *(p.16)* was in danger from the 1590s. Robert Dudley died in 1588, followed by Walsingham in 1590 and Cecil in 1598. This meant the patronage system began to fall apart as her trusted advisers disappeared.
- A new generation of ambitious politicians emerged following the deaths of the old ones. This caused unrest in the council, led by William Cecil's son, Robert Cecil, and Robert Devereux, the 2nd Earl of Essex.
- Robert Cecil took on an increasing workload as his father aged, and this made Essex jealous.
- Essex and the queen argued after she became increasingly annoyed by his actions and his secret marriage *(p.19)*. It resulted in the queen punching him and banishing him from court.
- Essex was told to defeat a rebellion in Ireland, but instead went against the queen's orders and made peace.
- When Essex returned from Ireland, he learned Cecil had been promoted. He burst into Elizabeth's chambers before she was wigged or gowned, for which he was put on house arrest and lost all jobs and monopolies.

What happened during the Essex rebellion?

Under arrest, Essex gathered 300 supporters and rumours of treason began to spread. Four Privy Council members went to question him and he held them hostage. He then proceeded to march on London to capture the queen.

Why did people desert the Essex rebellion?

Londoners were unimpressed and most of his supporters eventually deserted him. Essex found his route blocked, returned home and surrendered.

What was the result of the Essex rebellion?

Essex was accused of being a traitor and was executed in the Tower of London in 1601.

What was the importance of the Essex rebellion?

The rebellion was important for many reasons:
- It showed Elizabeth's control over her kingdom was fading as she couldn't always rely on the loyalty of those close to her.

- ✓ It showed some of the most powerful people in the kingdom were willing to disrespect her.
- ✓ It demonstrated how the system of patronage was breaking down as the rebellion would not have happened at the beginning of Elizabeth's reign. *(p.16)*
- ✓ Despite the negatives, it also showed Elizabeth was still relatively strong as Essex was only able to muster 300 supporters.

> **DID YOU KNOW?**
>
> **He was an unexpected choice for a rebel!**
> Devereux's mother married Robert Dudley, a close friend and favourite of Elizabeth I's, making him an unlikely pick to start a rebellion.

ELIZABETH'S PROBLEMS IN THE 1590S

The final phase of Elizabeth I's reign is regarded as a period of crisis, marred by political strife, economic strain and a series of draining wars on the continent and in Ireland. The combination of an ageing and indecisive queen, coupled with clashing personalities at court, resulted in political stagnation.

What were the years of decline?

The 1590s were seen as the years of decline for Elizabeth. Towards the end of her reign she found it harder to resolve problems.

What problems did Elizabeth face in the 1590s?

Elizabeth faced several challenges in the 1590s:

- ✓ Ireland became more challenging to govern, and this period saw the Nine Years War.
- ✓ The Earl of Essex, a member of the royal court, led a rebellion against Elizabeth.
- ✓ Elizabeth's closest and oldest advisers, such as Walsingham, were beginning to die.
- ✓ There was a severe outbreak of the plague in 1593.
- ✓ Elizabeth was becoming increasingly ill and had not ensured her succession.

> **DID YOU KNOW?**
>
> **The plague returned!**
> In December 1592–93, the plague broke out in London again. Over 19,000 deaths were recorded in the city and its surrounding parishes over the next 12 months.

ELIZABETHAN SOCIETY

Elizabethan England had four main classes: the Nobility, the Gentry, the Yeomanry, and the Poor. A person's class determined how they could dress, where they could live, and the kinds of jobs people and their children could get

How was Elizabethan society structured?

Society was extremely hierarchical, and was classified in medieval Christianity's Great Chain of Being, making it difficult to move social groups. Its structure differed between the countryside and the towns.

What was Elizabethan society like in the countryside?

90% of the population lived in the countryside. Society was structured so:
- At the top of the social structure was the monarch.
- Below the monarch was the nobility.
- Then it was the gentry.
- Then it was the yeomen, who were the lesser gentry.
- Below them were the tenant farmers, who rented their land from the yeomen or the gentry.
- Then it was the labouring poor, who owned no land.
- At the bottom of the structure were the homeless and vagabonds.

What was Elizabethan society like in the towns?

10% of the population lived in towns, where the hierarchy was based on how wealthy you were. The structure was as follows:
- The monarch and nobility were at the top of the social structure.
- They were followed by the merchants and professionals.
- Business owners and craftsmen were beneath them.
- Then it was the labourers.
- At the bottom were the homeless and the unemployed.

Who were the nobility in Elizabethan society?

The nobility were the most respected members of society and they sometime held titles such as duke, earl and baron. On average they earned £6,000 a year and were usually born into the position.

Who were the gentry in Elizabethan society?

The gentry earned between £10 to £200 a year. They had significant influence and power as some held positions as justices of the peace or served in Parliament. The numbers of gentry grew during Elizabeth's reign *(p.16)*, as did their power.

Why was fashion important in Elizabethan society?

Fashion was incredibly important. Women of the elite often paired fine clothes with whitened faces, to show they didn't have to work outside. A key element of fashion was the elaborate ruff worn around the neck.

> **DID YOU KNOW?**
>
> **The population of England increased dramatically during the Elizabethan period.**
> In 1558 the population was around 2.8 million but by 1603 it had increased to 4 million.

A 'GOLDEN AGE'

The Elizabethan period is known for its many different discoveries and achievements, leading to it being known as a 'Golden Age'.

What was the 'golden age' during Elizabethan times?

Elizabeth's reign *(p.16)* was seen as a 'golden age' of culture and exploration *(p.40)*.

Why was Elizabeth's reign considered a 'golden age'?

Elizabeth's reign *(p.16)* could be considered a 'golden age' because of the following:

- ☑ Theatre *(p.25)* was flourishing and becoming popular. Shakespeare wrote many of his famous plays during this era.
- ☑ England defeated the Spanish Armada *(p.59)* in 1588.
- ☑ The English economy improved.
- ☑ Drake circumnavigated the globe.
- ☑ Exploration *(p.40)* brought many discoveries back to England, such as spices and new foods.
- ☑ Elizabeth authorised the colonisation of the New World.

Did the golden age exist under Elizabeth?

It is debatable just how 'golden' the age was. Here are arguments for and against:

- ☑ It can be considered golden because of how culture and exploration *(p.40)* appeared to be flourishing.
- ☑ On the other hand, poverty *(p.33)* and religious dissent were very common. Elizabeth used the terms 'golden age' and 'Gloriana' as propaganda to bolster support.

> **DID YOU KNOW?**
>
> **This period is also known for the birth of the English witch craze!**
> The Elizabethans came up with two ways to protect themselves from evil witches. They placed dead cats into buildings above door frames to ward off the evil witches and their spirits, and created 'witch bottles' if they believed they were cursed. These were sealed with the victim's urine, hair, herbs, needles and pins, and represented the witch's bladder. The bottles were then heated over a fire to remove the curse from the victim.

ELIZABETHAN THEATRE

Theatre became more popular and was one of the main forms of entertainment - there were many famous playwrights including Shakespeare, Burbage and Marlowe at this time.

What was Elizabethan theatre like?
During Elizabeth I's reign *(p.16)*, both rich and poor enjoyed visits to the theatre. Audiences loved the theatre and many playwrights became very successful, including William Shakespeare.

How did Elizabethan theatre change over time?
During Elizabeth's reign *(p.16)*, theatre changed:
- At the beginning of her reign a trip to the theatre usually meant visiting an inn or watching a performance in a yard.
- In 1576, James Burbage built the first playhouse in London, called The Theatre. It included works by young playwrights from Oxford and Cambridge universities.
- Theatre became more popular as it became affordable for everyone.
- Christopher Marlowe rose to fame by writing many popular plays, such as 'Dr Faustus'.
- In 1592, Shakespeare wrote his first play, 'Henry VI, Part I'. Altogether, he wrote 38 plays and is one of the world's most celebrated playwrights.
- By the end of Elizabeth's reign *(p.16)* a number of purpose-built theatres, like The Globe, existed.

How was Elizabethan theatre funded?
Actors and companies were usually funded by patrons. Patrons would have companies named after themselves.

What was the role of theatre companies in Elizabethan theatre?
Companies of actors usually performed the plays. Some famous companies were The Lord Chamberlain's Men and The Admiral's Men.

Who were the actors in Elizabethan theatre?
Acting was a male-only profession. Actors such as William Kempe and Richard Burbage were particularly famous and performed many roles.

Who was the main playwright in Elizabethan theatre?
Shakespeare began writing his plays during Elizabethan times *(p.16)*. His plays always voiced support for the queen and the Tudor monarchy.

What are some examples of Elizabethan plays?
There were many famous plays performed during this time, but here are some of the most notable:
- The Spanish Tragedy, by Thomas Kyd.
- The Jew of Malta, by Christopher Marlowe.
- Richard III, by William Shakespeare.

Why was Elizabethan theatre popular?
The theatre was popular because it was affordable and accessible to everyone, exciting to watch, and also served as a social occasion.

Why was there opposition to Elizabethan theatre?
There were three main reasons why some people opposed the theatre.

- Puritans *(p.51)* believed the theatre was sinful and distracted people from prayer.
- Some people believed that large crowds could lead to the spread of disease.
- Some people saw the theatre as dangerous, as many of the audience were drunk and crimes were committed.

How was Elizabethan theatre used as propaganda?

There are a few examples of how Elizabeth used the theatre as propaganda:

- Plays would often be used for propaganda. For example, A Larum for London showed Spanish soldiers killing civilians. This was performed during the time that England and Spain were at war.
- Elizabeth approved plays she agreed with and banned those with which she did not.

How was Elizabethan theatre used to stop social mobility?

There are two ways in which social mobility was prevented:

- Social mobility was prevented as people had an affordable leisure activity that made them content with their lives.
- Plays about the Great Chain of Being told people that if you changed the order of the universe then there would be chaos.

> **DID YOU KNOW?**
>
> **Shakespeare took advantage of the growth in the arts.**
>
> Queen Elizabeth put a lot of money into London theatre and arts, building the first theatres and sponsoring productions. Shakespeare himself grew up and then benefitted from this, even publishing his first play, 'Henry IV', near the end of her reign.

THE GLOBE - HISTORIC ENVIRONMENT

The original Globe was an Elizabethan theatre which opened in autumn 1599 in Southwark, on the south bank of the Thames.

What was the Globe Theatre?

The Globe Theatre was built by Shakespeare's theatre *(p.25)* company in 1599 in Southwark, London. It was three storeys high and could hold up to 3,000 spectators.

How was the Globe Theatre structured?

The inside of the Globe Theatre was structured to reflect the social hierarchy of Elizabethan society *(p.23)*.

- The Lords' Rooms were the most expensive seats in the house and cost around 5 pence.
- The balconies to the left and right of the stage were the Gentlemen's Rooms. These cost around 4 pence.
- The galleries were seated sections covered by a roof and were for richer members of the audience.
- The pit was where ordinary people stood to watch the performance. The audience in this section heckled the actors.

> **DID YOU KNOW?**
>
> **You can still visit the Globe!**
> You can visit Shakespeare's Globe, a reconstruction of the original Elizabethan playhouse in London for which William Shakespeare wrote his plays.

ELIZABETHAN ARCHITECTURE

Striking effects included overhanging first floors, pillared porches and dormer windows.

What was Elizabethan architecture like?

The rich were very keen to show off their wealth and power. One way of doing this was through the architecture of their stately homes.

How was Elizabethan architecture possible?

The Dissolution of the Monasteries under Henry VIII freed up about a quarter of all land in England. This was now available for the rich to purchase.

What was the Great Rebuilding in Elizabethan architecture?

Building during Elizabeth's reign *(p.16)* was known as the Great Rebuilding. It celebrated a desire among the wealthy to show houses at their best.

What was the external architecture like on Elizabethan buildings?

There were 3 things that characterised the external design of Elizabethan homes.
- They were inspired by Italian Renaissance architecture.
- Many houses had large mullioned windows. These were large windows made up of many small panes of glass, divided by supports.
- Some manor houses were not classically influenced and were still made using wattle and daub.

What was the architecture like inside Elizabethan buildings?

There were 3 things that characterised the internal design of Elizabethan homes.
- Rooms were very well lit due to the large and extensive windows.
- Bedrooms were placed upstairs for the first time.
- There were long galleries for entertainment.

What was Robert Smythson's contribution to Elizabethan architecture?

Robert Smythson was a leading architect. He designed and built Longleat House and Hardwick Hall *(p.28)*.

How did Elizabethan architecture show the prosperity of its owners?

Architecture was used to display the prosperity of its owners in several ways:
- There was a new culture of personal comfort, meaning a country house was not the communal centre of a village, but a private residence for a cultured noble.

- ☑ It was fashionable to be inspired by ancient civilisations as it demonstrated a cultured mind.
- ☑ Expensive materials were used to show off an individual's wealth.
- ☑ A lot of glass was used on both the exterior and interior of a house to show off the owner's wealth.

> **DID YOU KNOW?**
>
> **The Elizabethans loved a chimney!**
> Chimney stacks in Elizabethan England reflect the Renaissance, which influenced a great deal of architecture during this period. Chimneys were often built to resemble classical columns and were square in section, as opposed to the twisting corkscrews of the Tudor years.

HARDWICK HALL - HISTORIC ENVIRONMENT

Bess - or rather Elizabeth, Countess of Shrewsbury - built one of the most imposing Elizabethan houses in the country at Hardwick. It was a testament to her ambition, power, and wealth.

What was Hardwick Hall?

Many great houses such as Hardwick Hall were built during Elizabeth's reign *(p.16)*. They houses were designed to not only demonstrate the wealth of their owners, but also to show they were cultured and fashionable.

Where was Hardwick Hall?

Hardwick Hall was built in Derbyshire.

Who is Bess of Hardwick Hall?

Elizabeth Cavendish, known as Bess of Hardwick, was the richest woman in England after the Queen.

How was Hardwick Hall designed?

Hardwick Hall has many features that make it immediately recognisable.

- ☑ Hardwick Hall was designed for appearance rather than security. It has been described as having more window than wall.
- ☑ Its 46 rooms demonstrate the wealth of the owner.
- ☑ At the top of the house, on the turrets, are the letters 'E' and 'S'. These stand for Elizabeth of Shrewsbury and were a display of Bess of Hardwick's wealth.

How does Hardwick Hall reflect the gentry?

Hardwick Hall reflects the gentry of the time in a number of ways:

- ☑ The gentry was becoming increasingly wealthy and able to afford more expensive things.
- ☑ Bess of Hardwick Hall was born into the gentry but increased her status and power through her four marriages.
- ☑ The materials used to build Hardwick Hall were expensive and often imported from abroad.
- ☑ The entire building is an extravagant showcase of wealth and power.

> **DID YOU KNOW?**
>
> **Bess was ahead of the times!**
> Hardwick Hall was a radical modern mansion, drawing on the latest Italian innovations in house design.

KENILWORTH CASTLE - ROBERT DUDLEY

Dudley was one of Elizabeth's closest advisors and the earl of Leicester. Many also believe he was Elizabeth's lover.

Who was Robert Dudley?
Robert Dudley was the Earl of Leicester and was considered the favourite of Queen Elizabeth *(p.14)*.

When did Robert Dudley join the Privy Council?
He was appointed to the Privy Council in October 1562.

Who was Robert Dudley's father?
Robert Dudley's father was John Dudley, who was executed in 1553 for attempting to oppose Mary I's succession.

What was Robert Dudley's family like?
The Dudleys were very proud of their ancestry and would display their family emblem wherever possible. They were also very close and loyal to each other.

What was the controversy surrounding Robert Dudley?
Robert Dudley was a potential marriage *(p.19)* suitor for Elizabeth. However, his first wife, Amy Robsart, was found dead at Cumnor Place after apparently falling down the stairs. Some believed Dudley was involved in her death.

What was Robert Dudley's relationship with Elizabeth like?
Elizabeth and Dudley's relationship changed over time:
- ☑ Dudley was born in 1532 and Elizabeth in 1533. They had known each other since they were children.
- ☑ They befriended each other during the reign of Mary I, when they were both under threat.
- ☑ When Elizabeth came to the throne she immediately appointed Dudley as Master of the Horse. He assisted the queen whenever they went riding.
- ☑ Despite Dudley being married *(p.19)* already, there were rumours about the two of them being lovers.
- ☑ In 1560 his wife died in suspicious circumstances. Many thought this was his chance to marry *(p.19)* the queen, but lingering suspicions over his involvement meant Elizabeth could never marry him.
- ☑ Elizabeth gifted him Kenilworth Castle *(p.30)* in 1563, and a year later gave him the title Earl of Leicester.
- ☑ In 1573 he was rumoured to have married *(p.19)* Lady Sheffield. The two did have an affair and she bore him a son.
- ☑ In 1578 he privately married *(p.19)* the queen's cousin, Lettice Knollys, which made Elizabeth furious.
- ☑ Despite this, they reconciled their friendship and remained friends until Dudley's death in 1588.

> **DID YOU KNOW?**
>
> **Dudley caused Elizabeth some scandal!**
> When the wife of Robert Dudley (with whom some believe Elizabeth was romantically involved) was found dead at the bottom of her own stairs, Dudley was suspected of arranging her murder so he could marry the queen.

KENILWORTH CASTLE - HISTORIC ENVIRONMENT

In 1563 Elizabeth I granted Kenilworth Castle to Robert Dudley, Earl of Leicester, who transformed it into a magnificent palace. He famously entertained the queen there for 19 days in 1575.

What was Kenilworth Castle?
Kenilworth Castle was a royal castle located in the Warwickshire town of the same name.

When was Kenilworth Castle built?
Kenilworth Castle was built in the 1120s.

Who built Kenilworth Castle?
It was built by Geoffrey de Clinton.

What is the history of Kenilworth Castle?
Kenilworth Castle has changed over time:
- In the early 13th century the castle was extended by King John, who added outer walls and a lake to help defend the fortress.
- Later in the century, the castle faced a 6-month long siege.
- In the 14th century, John of Gaunt developed the castle into a palace which included apartments and the great hall.
- In 1563 the castle was granted to Robert Dudley, who continued its development as a palace used for festivities and the royal court.
- The castle's fortifications were dismantled after the civil war in 1650 and it was left to go to ruin.

How did Robert Dudley change Kenilworth Castle?
Dudley made many significant changes to the design of Kenilworth Castle:
- He added a gatehouse in 1570.
- He built a bedchamber for Elizabeth I *(p.14)*.
- He built a gallery for Elizabeth I *(p.14)*.
- He also built her a withdrawing chamber.
- He also designed a magnificent garden.

How did Dudley change the gatehouse at Kenilworth Castle?
This was intended as the castle's new grand entrance, as it was wide enough for carriages to pass through and also had accommodation on two floors.

How did Dudley change the gardens at Kenilworth Castle?

Dudley designed an Italian-style private garden for the queen. It included a fountain of the Greek god, Atlas, a 20-foot aviary, and many different flowers - some of which were new to England.

How did Dudley change the bedchamber at Kenilworth Castle?

Elizabeth's bedchamber was positioned on the east side, with a substantial fireplace and large bay window.

Why did Dudley change Kenilworth Castle?

There are many possible reasons why Dudley made the changes to Kenilworth:

- [x] To impress Elizabeth.
- [x] To show off his status.
- [x] As a legacy to his family.
- [x] To persuade Elizabeth to marry *(p.19)* him.
- [x] To show he understood new fashions and trends.
- [x] As somewhere for Elizabeth to stay on her progresses.

When did Elizabeth visit Kenilworth Castle?

The queen visited the castle four times during her progresses. In 1575 she stayed for a total of 19 days.

Why did Elizabeth go on progresses to Kenilworth Castle?

There were several reasons Elizabeth went on progresses:

- [x] It allowed her to be seen frequently by her subjects.
- [x] She could flatter and cultivate the nobles she stayed with.
- [x] The progresses allowed Elizabeth to live in luxury while not spending money, as the nobility desperately wanted to impress her.
- [x] They gave the royal court an excuse to escape from the capital at times when the plague was rife.

What events happened at Kenilworth Castle in 1575?

During the royal progress to Kenilworth Castle in 1575, Dudley tried to impress the queen in a number of ways:

- [x] The queen was greeted by actors delivering speeches of welcome and bearing gifts, including the keys to the castle.
- [x] Dancing - one of Elizabeth's favourite pastimes - took place frequently during this progress.
- [x] There were elaborate banquets where guests consumed up to 40 barrels of beer and 16 barrels of wine per day.
- [x] There were firework displays that were said to be heard from 20 miles away.

DID YOU KNOW?

The ghost of Elizabeth haunts an English castle!

Castles were an especially common place for people to see ghosts. The ghost of Queen Elizabeth I is reported to haunt Windsor Castle to this day.

ELIZABETHAN LEISURE

People from all social classes enjoyed some sort of leisure or pastime activities - these range from drinking and gambling to studying music and hawking.

What did people do for leisure during Elizabethan times?
There were very different leisure activities for the higher levels of society and those of the lower levels.

What were the leisure activities for the nobles during Elizabeth's rule?
The invention of the printing press meant many gentlemen were involved in intellectual culture, including reading the classics and studying music. They also indulged in hunting and hawking. These sports were expensive and required a lot of free time.

What were the leisure activities for most people during Elizabeth's rule?
Most people worked from Monday to Saturday and went to church on Sunday. The vast majority often became involved in leisure activities such as drinking, gambling, cockfighting and playing cards.

Was football a leisure activity in Elizabethan times?
Local teams would play *(p.25)* against each other, using an inflated pig's bladder as the ball. There could be hundreds of players on a team.

DID YOU KNOW?

The Elizabethans played tennis!
'Real tennis' was an indoor game played by upper class men. It was a cross between modern tennis and squash.

ELIZABETHAN EDUCATION

Education in the Elizabethan age was very different depending on your upbringing and social class.

What was education like during Elizabeth I's reign?
Elizabethans saw education as an important part of life and a way to climb the social ladder. The main purpose of education was to teach children appropriate behaviour and to make them useful members of society.

What was education like for girls in Elizabethan England?
Education was a luxury for most people and those who attended schools were mainly boys from wealthier society. Hardly any girls attended school.

What was education like for young children in Elizabethan England?
Children were taught about behaviour and religion at home. At age six, children went to Sunday school. Rich children learned with the help of private tutors, and poor children were trained in housekeeping and basic manual labour.

How were petty schools involved with education in Elizabethan England?
Petty schools (or dame schools) taught maths, reading, and writing. There was no official curriculum and no classes. Children were not split into year groups. They started at the age of six, became literate and then left.

How were grammar schools involved with education in Elizabethan England?
Grammar schools were private schools for boys from middle class families. The main topic taught was Latin, but students also learned history and philosophy.

How was the horn book used in education in Elizabethan England?
This was the most important tool used in grammar schools. A horn book was a piece of parchment usually pasted to a small wooden board. The horn book displayed the alphabet in both small letters and capital letters.

What was education like for the nobility in Elizabethan England?
Children of the nobility were often taught at home. They would be taught foreign languages, history and politics. Boys would be taught fencing, swimming and other sports; girls would be taught needlework and music.

What was higher education like in Elizabethan England?
A university degree was seen as a route to the professions for those who were not nobles. The two universities in England were Oxford and Cambridge.

What did boys do if they could not afford university in Elizabethan England?
Most boys began an apprenticeship after grammar school because they could not afford to attend university.

> **DID YOU KNOW?**
>
> **Many people in Elizabethan England were illiterate.**
>
> In 1500, it was estimated only 10% of males and 1% of females were literate. To prove your literacy you only had to write your name. If only GCSE English was that easy....

POVERTY IN ELIZABETHAN ENGLAND
During Elizabeth's reign, an increasing population helped caused a simultaneous increase in the amount of those living in poverty.

What was life like for the very poor in Elizabethan England?
During the Elizabethan period, life could be very hard for ordinary people and poverty could be extreme. Unlike now, there was no welfare system or support for those who needed it.

How did people view poverty in Elizabethan times?
People in Elizabethan times *(p.16)* had a number of beliefs about poverty.
- They believed that some people, such as the old and sick, could not help being in poverty and deserved help. These were called the 'deserving poor'.

- ☑ They believed that other people were poor because they were feckless and lazy. These were known as the 'undeserving poor' or 'sturdy beggars'.
- ☑ They believed in the 'Chain of Being', which stated that it was important for everyone to remain in their own place in society.

What were the main causes of poverty in Elizabethan times?

There were seven main causes of poverty in Elizabethan England *(p.16)*. You can remember these more easily by using the acronym WHIPPED, which stands for the following:

- ☑ War increased taxes for ordinary people as it was very expensive. Moreover, when war was over, many were left unemployed.
- ☑ Harvests in England were bad between 1594 and 1598, which led to food shortages. Some people died of starvation.
- ☑ Inflation was particularly bad during this period. The bad harvests drove up food price, especially for grain. This was made worse as wages did not increase as quickly as the price of goods.
- ☑ Population - the number of people in England grew from 2.8 to 4 million during this period.
- ☑ Policies - previous monarchs' policies left many people without work. Henry VIII closed the monasteries, which caused unemployment and impacted the poor as these were the places where they went for medical treatment when they were sick.
- ☑ Enclosure farming meant people were farming sheep rather than crops. This required fewer workers.
- ☑ Diseases such as the plague and smallpox left families without a wage earner.

> **DID YOU KNOW?**
>
> **They drank alcohol all day!**
> People who lived in the country would drink fresh water, but most British people in Elizabethan England drank cider, wine, ale or cider instead as the water was so unclean.

PAUPERS AND POVERTY

Paupers were at the bottom of the 'Chain of Being'. However, changing attitudes and understanding meant people began to pity them and brought about change.

Who were the paupers?

People who didn't have jobs in Elizabethan society *(p.23)* were called paupers. Paupers were at the bottom of the social ladder.

What was done to help the paupers during Elizabeth's rule?

People began to understand that paupers were not to necessarily to blame for their own poverty *(p.33)*. Charities set up to assist the poor became more common.

What kind of paupers were vagabonds during Elizabeth's rule?

The wandering poor were known as vagabonds. They usually relied on begging to survive.

What were the laws against paupers during Elizabeth's rule?

There were two acts introduced to reduce begging.

- The Vagabonds Act 1572.
- The Act for the Relief of the Poor 1576.

How did the Vagabonds Act 1572 affect paupers?

The Vagabonds Act 1572 was intended to punish vagabonds in the following ways:
- Beggars were whipped in public.
- If beggars were caught more than once, they had a hole burned in their ear.
- Further offences led to hanging.

How did the Act for the Relief of the Poor 1576 help paupers?

The Act for the Relief of the Poor 1576 was intended to help solve the problem of unemployment in the following ways:
- Each town was required to provide work for the unemployed.
- People refusing to pay the poor rate were punished.
- Houses of correction were built in each county.

> **DID YOU KNOW?**
> **Clothes were also used to help differentiate classes!**
> Elizabethan laws even dictated what kind and colour of clothes each class could wear so they could be immediately identified.

RESPONSE TO THE POOR

The Elizabethan Poor Law was enacted in 1601, making local governments responsible for providing work and aid for unemployed persons, and especially for children and the aged.

How were poor people treated in Elizabethan times?

During the Elizabethan period, attitudes towards the poor began to change due to the growth of poverty *(p.33)*. This is because people were beginning to understand some people couldn't help their situations.

How did almshouses affect the poor?

Almshouses, providing accommodation for those in need, were opened during this period.

How were the poor categorised during Elizabethan times?

Initially, the poor were categorised depending on what they did or what they couldn't do.
- The deserving poor were people who were able-bodied and trying to help themselves, but who couldn't find work.
- The undeserving poor were people who were thought to be able to work but chose not to. They were seen as lazy.

> **DID YOU KNOW?**
>
> **The Elizabethan Poor Law was the first of its kind!**
> The 1601 Poor Law signalled an important progression from private charity to welfare state, where the care and supervision of the poor was embodied in law and integral to the management of each town.

POOR LAWS

During the reign of Elizabeth I, legislation was passed to deal with the increasing problem of raising and administering poor relief.

What was the Poor Law?
The Poor Law was a law that taxed the wealthy in order to pay for the care of the poor.

Why was the Poor Law introduced?
There were four main reasons why Elizabeth introduced the Poor Laws.
- There were fears the social order might be threatened if the growing number of poor started a rebellion.
- There was a risk vagabonds and beggars might turn to crime.
- There were fears the poor were spreading disease.
- The landowners were giving more to the poor.

What were the main provisions of the Poor Law?
There were four main provisions in the Poor Law.
- Justices of the peace had to appoint four overseers of the poor in each parish.
- Almshouses were provided for the old or sick to work in.
- Beggars had to be returned to their place of birth or put into a house of correction.
- A poor rate was charged to pay for these measures.

How were the poor divided under the new Poor Law?
The poor were divided into three groups.
- The helpless poor were the sick and old. They were provided with food to live on and placed in almshouses where they could be cared for.
- The able-bodied poor were those who were considered fit, including children. They were expected to work. They were given food and drink as payment, and sometimes somewhere to sleep.
- The idle poor were seen as lazy and were whipped. They were also sent to a house of correction where they would be forced to work.

What three towns was the Poor Law based on?
Elizabeth's government *(p.16)* based the Poor Law on its research of three main cities.
- York was a very prosperous city with a large number of beggars. The council in York put many of those beggars to work, which helped boost industry. Those who refused were sent to the houses of correction.

- Ipswich introduced a licensing system for beggars and increased support for the poor in 1569. There were hospitals set up specifically to help the old and sick who could not afford treatment.
- Norwich separated its poor into two categories: 'idle poor' and 'unfortunate poor'. The idle poor were given work, while the unfortunate poor were given food and other forms of support.

What were the positives to come out of the Poor Law?

There were several positive outcomes achieved by the Poor Law.

- The Poor Law continued to recognise people who wanted to work but were unable to find employment.
- The Poor Law filled the 'care' gap that had been left by the monasteries a generation earlier.
- No rebellion caused by poverty *(p.33)* occurred during Elizabeth's reign *(p.16)*. In this sense, the laws achieved their main aim; social order was preserved.
- The Poor Law was an important milestone. For the first time in England, the government took direct responsibility for the welfare of the people.
- Despite criticism, the Poor Law remained in effect until it was reformed in 1834.
- Orphans had apprenticeships, paid for by the parish, so they learned a trade. Almshouses were also provided for the old and ill to live in and they could receive handouts of money, food, and clothing. This was called outdoor relief.
- Instances of begging seemed to decrease.
- Although charitable giving was still encouraged, the new Poor Law stated that everyone had to pay towards a local poor rate, making it fair.

What were the negatives to come out of the Poor Law?

There were three main negative outcomes of the Poor Law.

- Some have argued that the extent of poverty *(p.33)* in this period has been wildly exaggerated, so giving the Elizabethan Poor Law more credit than it deserves.
- There was still a strong belief that many of those in poverty *(p.33)* were lazy and much of the legislation focused on preventing laziness by punishing those who were able, but unwilling, to work.
- Poverty *(p.33)* continued to grow after the Poor Law was introduced. As each area was responsible for its own poor, there were arguments over which area paupers belonged to. Without a clear home, some paupers were simply sent from one area to another.

> **DID YOU KNOW?**
>
> **It took 200 years for Poor Laws to change.**
> The Poor Laws were finally reviewed in 1834. Many of the debates about who deserved to be helped and who did not were revisited and argued about at this time.

DRAKE - DISCOVERIES

Sir Francis Drake was the most famous mariner of the Elizabethan age and earned a reputation for his privateering, or piracy, against Spanish ships and possessions.

Who was Sir Francis Drake?

Francis Drake was the first Englishman to travel around the globe. His voyage included raiding Spanish ports in the Americas, and losing several ships from his fleet in storms. He was knighted on his return.

When was Sir Francis Drake's voyage?
Sir Francis Drake left Plymouth to start his most famous voyage on December 13th, 1577.

What was Sir Francis Drake's importance?
There are 3 main reasons why Drake was important.
- He brought back considerable wealth from his travels.
- The knighthood he received encouraged more British sailors.
- He was key to the defeat of the Spanish Armada (p.59).

What was important about Sir Francis Drake's circumnavigation of the world?
Drake's circumnavigation of the globe between 1577-1580 was important for 5 reasons.
- The navy (p.58) was expanded and seen as a big threat by other countries - its success garnered it an even more fearsome reputation.
- Trade was improved - for example, by signing a trade treaty with the Spice Islands (now the Maluku Islands) in Indonesia which allowed English merchants to trade in valuable spices.
- New discoveries were made, such as finding that Java was an island. This corrected an earlier geographical error made by Dutch explorers, who had believed it was connected to a continent.
- Drake achieved personal glory by capturing the Spanish ship, the Nuestra Señora de la Concepcion, nicknamed Cacafuego. This was Drake's most famous prize, as it carried 362,000 pesos in silver and gold.
- Drake returned with an estimated £400,000 worth of treasure captured from the Spanish - amounting to about £200 million in today's money. The queen received a half-share of the money, which was more than her entire income for the whole year.

What was Elizabeth's interest in Sir Francis Drake's trip?
Elizabeth took a large part of the treasure that Drake brought home from his journey in order to increase the country's riches.

DID YOU KNOW?

You can visit a full scale reconstruction of the ship in which Drake circumnavigated the globe!

The Golden Hind reconstruction is located in London and you can jump aboard for just a few pounds. The ship actually did its own circumnavigation of the globe over the course of five years in the 1970s!

HAWKINS - DISCOVERIES

John Hawkins was key to developing the Elizabethan navy. He served as a vice-admiral against the Spanish Armada and was knighted for his courage after the defeat of the Spanish.

Who was John Hawkins?
Sir John Hawkins was an Elizabethan adventurer who helped develop England's navy (p.58). He was also the first English slave trader.

What did John Hawkins do?
He was notable for several reasons:
- He was responsible for building up the Royal Navy *(p.58)*.
- He was a military leader and played a major role in defeating the Spanish Armada *(p.59)*.
- He was a successful privateer, like Francis Drake.
- In 1562 he became involved in the slave trade.

> **DID YOU KNOW?**
>
> **He played a big part in the rise of the slave trade!**
> In 1562, Hawkins became the first Englishman to capture people in Sierra Leone and sell them as slaves to Spanish settlers in the Caribbean.

RALEIGH - DISCOVERIES

Sir Walter Raleigh was an English adventurer, writer, and nobleman who was knighted in 1585 and became Captain of the Guard. He organised 3 major expeditions to America, including the ill-fated Roanoke settlement.

Who was Sir Walter Raleigh?
Sir Walter Raleigh was very loyal to Queen Elizabeth *(p.14)* I. He became a favourite of the queen after fighting Catholic rebels and exploring parts of North and South America.

What did Walter Raleigh do in the New World?
In 1584, Raleigh had permission to explore and colonise any land not already ruled by a Christian. As a result a colony was established at Roanoke, in what is now North Carolina in the United States. The initial colony failed and the starving colonists returned to England.

What happened to the colony Sir Walter Raleigh set up?
After the first failed attempt, a second colony was established at Roanoke in 1587 but it couldn't produce enough food and faced hostility from a local tribe. On his return from a trip to England, the colony leader found everyone had disappeared with no trace of them left behind.

What happened to Sir Walter Raleigh?
Raleigh remained a favourite at court. However, in 1592, when Elizabeth discovered he had married *(p.19)* one of her ladies-in-waiting without asking for royal assent, Raleigh was banished from court and even briefly imprisoned.

What were the key events of Walter Raleigh's life?
There were several key events in Walter Raleigh's life.
- Raleigh fought for the Protestant Huguenots in France, during the French Wars of Religion, when he was only 15 years old.
- He also fought against the Catholics in Ireland when they rebelled against Elizabeth I. He was given land there as a reward.
- In 1584, Raleigh gained the queen's permission to establish England's first colony in America. The colony, known as Roanoke, was a failure.

- ☑ Raleigh explored Guiana in 1595, searching for 'El Dorado' - a legendary city of gold. He wrote a book about his travels on his return to England.

 What was Walter Raleigh's significance?

Walter Raleigh was a significant figure for several reasons:
- ☑ Although it was a failure, Roanoke was the first English colony in America. Raleigh inspired all those who followed him to establish subsequent colonies.
- ☑ Raleigh's book on his travels to Guiana inspired others to explore the world, leading to settlement and the eventual growth of the British Empire.

> **DID YOU KNOW?**
>
> **Walters ran in the family!**
> Walter's father was called Walter and when his son was born....you guessed it, Walter named him Walter.

NAVIGATION AND EXPLORATION

The Elizabethan period saw the major European powers engage in many voyages of discovery. The discovery of the Americas opened up new lands to explore.

 How was exploration possible?

Exploration of the globe could only be achieved through new technology.

 What was the Age of Discovery in the Elizabethan era?

Elizabeth's reign *(p.16)* was known as the Age of Discovery and Exploration.

Why did Elizabethan exploration happen?

There were many reasons for the expansion of Elizabethan exploration.
- ☑ England was seeking new trade partners in the Far East, such as India and China.
- ☑ Elizabeth wanted to be seen as powerful and exploration would boost her image.
- ☑ There had been drastic improvements in technology, which made navigation easier and ships better.
- ☑ Europeans were interested in overseas culture and goods.
- ☑ The Renaissance era led to an increase in scientific curiosity.

What was the circumnavigation during Elizabethan's exploration?

Sir Francis Drake was the leading explorer. Drake circumnavigated the globe between 1577 and 1580. The discoveries he made led to a completely new understanding of the world in England.

 How was the slave trade involved in Elizabethan exploration?

Throughout Elizabeth's reign *(p.16)*, England's involvement in the slave trade grew. Many more slave traders made a fortune by meeting the demand for slaves to work in the New World in the Americas. Sir Francis Drake and his second cousin, Sir John Hawkins *(p.38)*, made one of the first voyages to Africa and captured people to sell as slaves in the New World.

What were the negative outcomes of Elizabethan exploration?
Elizabeth's unofficial support for the explorers, or privateers, may have worsened relations with Philip II *(p.54)* of Spain.

What were the positive outcomes for England from Elizabethan exploration?
There were a few positive outcomes of the Age of Discovery.
- The Age of Discovery increased England's position as a global superpower.
- Drake and other privateers' actions helped to improve the English economy as any treasure taken had to be shared with the queen.
- England's empire was expanding due to colonisation.
- It led to improved geographical knowledge of the world.
- Trade links were established with new countries.

How were English ships used for exploration superior to other countries' vessels during Elizabeth's rule?
There were three main reasons why English ships were superior to others at the time.
- Ships at this time were built with new lateen (triangular) sails which made them faster and easier to steer.
- The astrolabe allowed sailors to judge how far north or south they were, and compasses allowed for navigation to be more accurate.
- Better defensive weapons made sailing through enemy and hostile waters much safer.

> **DID YOU KNOW?**
>
> **Discoveries led to the arrival of some of our favourite foods in the UK.**
>
> There are many items we now take for granted that were tasted for the first time in the Elizabethan era, such as tomatoes, chilli peppers, chocolate and avocados!

HENRY VIII AND THE REFORMATION
When Pope Clement VII refused to annul Henry's marriage to Catherine of Aragon so he could remarry, the English king declared in 1534 that he alone should be the final authority in matters relating to the Church.

What was Henry VIII's Reformation?
King Henry VIII decided in the 1530s to change the religion of England from Catholic to Protestant in order to help achieve his aims. This is known as the 'break from Rome'.

What was Henry VIII's reason for the Reformation?
There are three main reasons why Henry decided to split from the Roman Catholic church.
- He wanted to rid himself of his first wife, Catherine of Aragon, after she failed to produce a male heir to the throne to carry on the Tudor name. However, the pope refused to grant him a divorce.
- Henry had also fought a very expensive war with France and needed a way to pay his soldiers. If he closed all the Catholic monasteries and abbeys in England, he could take their wealth.

- Henry was power-hungry. He did not like the idea of the pope having authority in England and knew that if he could produce a male heir, then the Tudor name would carry on for years after his death.

What were the consequences of Henry VIII's Reformation?

There were four main consequences of the Reformation.

- Henry took the wealth of the English monasteries and became very rich.
- Many people did not agree with the Reformation. There were several rebellions, such as the Pilgrimage of Grace in 1536.
- The Protestant faith grew under Henry VIII.
- It led to a nation divided on religion, which would cause problems for his successors.

> **DID YOU KNOW?**
>
> **Henry VIII wasn't expected to become king.**
>
> His older brother Arthur was meant to become king and even married Catherine of Aragon in preparation. However, he died shortly after the wedding. This left Henry as next in line to the throne and in 1509 he became King of England. He also then married Catherine, his brother's widow!

EDWARD VI AND THE REFORMATION

Edward did not play an active part in controlling his reign. However, the dukes who were in charge took religious matters more seriously and continued to further break from Rome.

What was Edward VI's reformation?

Under Edward VI, the church became more Protestant.

How did Edward VI's Reformation affect priests?

Priests were allowed to marry *(p.19)* and the Book of Common Prayer, written in English, was published, which removed elements of the Catholic mass. Churches were no longer lavishly ornamented.

What was the impact of Edward VI's Reformation?

In 1549 there was a rebellion targeted against the Book of Common Prayer. However, it was defeated.

> **DID YOU KNOW?**
>
> **Catholics were still able to worship.**
>
> Many would attend church services and then had private Catholic services at home, or one family member would attend to avoid paying fines.

MARY I AND THE REFORMATION

Mary I tried vigorously to reverse the English Reformation, which had begun during the reign of her father, Henry VIII.

What was Mary I's reformation?
Mary was a devout Catholic and tried to turn England back to Catholicism.

How did Mary I's Reformation affect England?
Mary's Reformation affected life in England in a number of ways.
- The pope was restored as head of the church.
- The Latin mass was brought back.
- Bibles were produced in Latin again.
- In 1554, the country was officially reunited with Rome.

What was the impact of Mary I's Reformation?
Protestants were persecuted during Mary I's reign, with almost 300 executed.

DID YOU KNOW?

Mary was not allowed to attend her mother's funeral.
Following their divorce, Catherine was banished from court but refused to acknowledge Anne Boleyn as the new queen. Mary supported her mother, so when Catherine died in 1536, Mary was forbidden to be present at the funeral.

THE RELIGIOUS SETTLEMENT

Elizabeth I attempted to unite the country after the changes in religion under Henry VIII, Edward VI, and Mary I. The Religious Settlement was designed to settle the divide between Catholics and Protestants and address the differences in services and beliefs.

What was the Religious Settlement?
The Religious Settlement was an effort by Elizabeth I *(p.14)* to unite the country. It was intended to resolve the dispute between Catholics and Protestants. As a Protestant, Elizabeth had to tread carefully between both faiths to maintain unity.

Why was the Religious Settlement of 1559 necessary?
England was in religious turmoil and there were several problems Elizabeth needed to face when tackling the issue.
- Most people in Elizabethan England *(p.16)* were Catholic, but the majority of the government was Protestant.
- The most powerful countries in Europe were Catholic.
- Religious changes in the past had caused rebellions.
- Mary, Queen of Scots *(p.45)*, claimed she was the rightful Queen of England and many Catholics supported her.
- Elizabeth I *(p.14)* wanted the country to be united and didn't want people to be punished for their beliefs.
- Elizabeth I *(p.14)* needed a national church which most of her people would accept.

What differences between Catholics and Protestants caused the Religious Settlement?

Catholicism and Protestantism beliefs differed in many ways:
- Catholics believed the bible and church services should be in Latin.
- Protestants held services in English and had an English bible, making it more accessible.
- The pope is the head of the Catholic church.
- As national leader, Elizabeth I *(p.14)* was head of the Protestant church.
- Catholics worship saints while Protestants do not.
- Catholic priests cannot marry *(p.19)*, whereas Protestant clergy can.

How were the changes of the Religious Settlement implemented?

They were implemented in the Act of Uniformity and the Act of Supremacy of 1559.

What key changes to religion did the Religious Settlement introduce?

There were 4 important changes made by Elizabeth.
- The Act of Uniformity stated church services had to be in English, a new prayer book was to be used and the Bible was to be in English.
- The Protestant faith was re-established in England. Elizabeth worked hard through propaganda to link loyalty to her with loyalty to the Church.
- The Act of Supremacy named Elizabeth as supreme governor of the Church of England. All clergy had to swear an oath to her. Only a few refused, and they were sacked.
- Priests and the clergy were allowed to marry *(p.19)*.

What was the outcome of the Religious Settlement?

England became a more secular society. Protestantism was the official religion of England, but Catholicism was also accepted, instead of its followers being persecuted.

What was the reaction of the Catholics to the Religious Settlement?

England had been a Catholic nation under the rule of the previous monarch, Mary I. Catholics were not happy with the Religious Settlement.
- They were angry that Latin mass was banned, and many continued to hold this service with priests in secret. Some even refused to attend church as Elizabeth refused to strictly enforce the recusancy fines of 5p.
- More than anything, English Catholics still viewed the pope as the head of their church, not Elizabeth as supreme governor.
- On 27th April 1570, Pope Pius V excommunicated Elizabeth from the Catholic church in the papal bull. This lead to an increase in opposition from Catholics as they saw it as their duty to rise up against her.

What was the reaction of the Puritans to the Religious Settlement?

Puritans *(p.51)* were unhappy with the settlement as they believed that Elizabeth should have legislated for a truly radical Puritan church.

> **DID YOU KNOW?**
>
> **Many Catholic families would pray in secret. They would even offer to host Catholic priests in order to give mass.**
>
> Scared of the consequences if caught, many Catholic families built priest holes into their homes. These were false walls or hidden compartments where priests could hide if authorities came to search the house. Some led to the drainage system and priests sometimes had to hide in raw sewage for days on end!

ARRIVAL OF MARY, QUEEN OF SCOTS

Mary, Queen of Scots' arrival was a threat to Elizabeth's rule because she had two claims to the English throne. Elizabeth had converted England's official religion to Protestantism, leaving many Catholics disgruntled. Mary was a Catholic and many viewed her as their figurehead and a rightful replacement to the throne.

Who was Mary, Queen of Scots?

Mary, Queen of Scots, was Elizabeth's cousin. She became Queen of Scotland in 1542. In 1558 she married *(p.19)* the heir to the throne of France and was briefly the queen of two countries. Mary was also an heir to the English throne.

When did Mary, Queen of Scots, rule?

Mary became Queen of Scots in 1542. She was briefly Queen of France, from 1559 to 1560, before returning to Scotland. She fled to England in 1568, where she lived in captivity until her execution in 1587.

Why was Mary, Queen of Scots, a threat to Elizabeth?

There were five main reasons why Mary was a threat to Elizabeth, even before Mary's arrival in England in 1568.

- ☑ Mary's first husband was Lord Darnley. He had a claim to the English throne, which strengthened Mary's own.
- ☑ Mary had a son, which meant she had a possible heir.
- ☑ Mary, Queen of Scots, was married *(p.19)* to Francis II of France, which increased the risk of Scotland and France invading England. Mary could then become the Queen of England, too.
- ☑ Elizabeth did not have any children. Mary was her closest living relative, which made Mary next in line to the English throne.
- ☑ Because Mary, Queen of Scots, was Catholic, she was supported by those who wanted to restore Catholicism to England.

When did Mary, Queen of Scots flee Scotland to England?

In 1568 Mary, Queen of Scots, fled to England hoping for protection from her enemies in Scotland.

What was the reaction of Mary, Queen of Scots' supporters?

Mary's arrival in England increased Catholic resistance to Elizabeth. Mary was seen by Catholics as a rallying point and a figurehead for their rebellions.

How was Mary, Queen of Scots, treated by Elizabeth when she was in England?

Mary was held captive for 19 years at various locations in England until she was found guilty of plotting against Elizabeth and executed.

> **DID YOU KNOW?**
>
> **Elizabeth I never actually met her biggest rival!**
> Even though she has her imprisoned in England for many years, Elizabeth never met her cousin and rival, Mary, Queen of Scots.

THE NORTHERN REBELLION

The Northern Rebellion was an unsuccessful attempt by Catholic nobles from Northern England to depose Queen Elizabeth I of England and replace her with Mary, Queen of Scots.

What was the Northern Rebellion?
The Northern Rebellion was an attempt by Catholic nobles to overthrow Queen Elizabeth *(p.14)* and replace her with Mary, Queen of Scots *(p.45)*.

What was the Northern Rebellion known as?
This rebellion is also known as Norfolk's Rebellion and the Revolt of the Northern Earls.

When was the Northern Rebellion?
It happened in November 1569 after Mary, Queen of Scots *(p.45)*, arrived in England.

Why did the Northern Rebellion happen?
After Elizabeth's coronation, she faced a lot of opposition from Catholics who didn't believe she had the right to be queen.

- Many believed her father's marriage *(p.19)* to Anne Boleyn, her mother, was illegal because it broke the sacred laws of marriage due to his divorce from Catherine of Aragon.
- Mary's presence in the north of England, which was a hotbed of Catholic support, encouraged the Catholic nobles to attempt to take power through physical force.
- The Duke of Norfolk resented William Cecil's influence on the monarchy and was intent on increasing Catholic influence in the royal court.
- Previously influential northern Catholic nobles had lost power in the royal court under Elizabeth. They saw the restoration of Catholicism as a way to regain power.
- James Pilkington, a Protestant, was appointed Archbishop of Durham in 1561, and aimed to stamp out Catholicism in the north. His harsh treatment of Catholics increased support for a rebellion.

What happened during the Northern Rebellion?
There were many stages to this rebellion.

- Elizabeth prevented Thomas Howard, Duke of Norfolk, from marrying Mary, Queen of Scots *(p.45)*. Norfolk left the royal court without permission and headed north.
- Taking this as a sign, a group of northern lords led by Westmorland and Northumberland began the rebellion by holding an illegal Catholic mass in Durham Cathedral.
- Afterwards, they began to march south with around 4,600 men. Elizabeth struggled to raise an army to resist them.
- Eventually one of her loyal lords, the Earl of Sussex, raised an army and the rebels fled.

What were the results of the Northern Rebellion?

There were four important consequences of the revolt.

- ☑ The Revolt of the Northern Earls led to increased oppression of Catholics and greater government control in the north.
- ☑ Elizabeth quickly put Mary, Queen of Scots *(p.45)*, under house arrest and sent her to Coventry to secure her imprisonment.
- ☑ There were more than 450 executions of Catholics who had been involved in the revolt, including the Earl of Northumberland in 1572.
- ☑ The lack of support for the revolt reflected Elizabeth's popularity. However, because of this threat, Elizabeth passed treason laws that made any further Catholic threat to the monarch punishable by death.

> **DID YOU KNOW?**
>
> **Elizabeth was not happy with the rebellion, as you can imagine!**
> She even wrote to the Earl of Sussex after the rising was crushed, complaining that she hadn't heard of any executions by martial law!

THE PAPAL BULL

In 1570 the pope issued a Papal Bull of Excommunication against Elizabeth and actively encouraged plots against her.

What was the papal bull of 1570?

Elizabeth's response to the Northern Rebellion *(p.46)* of 1569, together with the growing religious divide, forced Pope Pius V to issue a decree in 1570. This declared Elizabeth was not a legitimate monarch and the people should not obey her.

How did the papal bull of 1570 affect Elizabeth?

Elizabeth was more vulnerable to rebellion and assassination as an illegitimate leader. However, the rebellion the pope had hoped for did not happen.

> **DID YOU KNOW?**
>
> **Elizabeth amended the law to try and persuade against any wrongdoing towards her.**
> In 1571, Parliament passed a law making it treason for anyone to claim Elizabeth was not the rightful Queen of England.

RIDOLFI

The Ridolfi plot was a plot in 1571 to assassinate Queen Elizabeth I of England and replace her with Mary, Queen of Scots. It was planned by Roberto Ridolfi, an international banker, who carried messages from Mary to Pope Pius V and Philip II of Spain, encouraging use of a Spanish army to invade England.

What was the Ridolfi plot?

In 1571, an Italian called Ridolfi planned a rebellion against Elizabeth. The plan was to stage an invasion from the Netherlands at the same time as another northern rebellion *(p.46)*. Elizabeth was to be murdered and replaced with Mary, Queen of Scots *(p.45)*.

Who was involved in the Ridolfi Plot?

There were 5 important participants in the Ridolfi plot.

- Thomas Howard, Duke of Norfolk.
- King Philip II *(p.54)*.
- Guerau de Espes del Valle, the Spanish ambassador to England.
- Pope Pius V.
- Mary, Queen of Scots *(p.45)*.

What was the impact of the Ridolfi Plot?

Elizabeth's advisers discovered the plot after intercepting Mary, Queen of Scots *(p.45)*' letters. This is what happened after:

- The Duke of Norfolk was executed.
- The Treasons Act of 1571 was passed in which it was detailed that anyone who said Elizabeth was not the rightful queen was a traitor.
- Recusants were now fined £20.
- Attempting to convert people to Catholicism was now classed as treason.

> **DID YOU KNOW?**
>
> **The plot was only discovered through the torture of one of Mary's associates.**
> Charles Baillie was tortured and eventually gave up the plot to harm Elizabeth.

THROCKMORTON

The Throckmorton Plot was a plan to utilise French and Spanish troops to oust Elizabeth and replace her with Mary, Queen of Scots. It was devised by Francis Throckmorton along with his brother, Thomas, and agents from Spain.

What was the Throckmorton Plot?

The Throckmorton Plot of 1583 was led by Sir Francis Throckmorton and aimed to replace Elizabeth with Mary, Queen of Scots *(p.45)*. The plotters planned the death of Elizabeth, followed by a French Catholic invasion and an uprising of English Catholics.

Who was involved in the Throckmorton Plot?

The plot involved:
- Francis Throckmorton.
- Bernardino de Mendoza, the Spanish ambassador to England.
- The French ambassador.
- Mary, Queen of Scots (p.45).

What was the outcome of the Throckmorton Plot?

One of the queen's spies in the French embassy revealed Throckmorton's plot. Throckmorton had conspired with the French and Spanish ambassadors and was executed.

What were the consequences of the Throckmorton Plot?

The Bond of Association was created. This was a document that committed to hunting down and executing anyone trying to overthrow or kill the queen. All English nobles and everyone in the royal court had to sign it.

> **DID YOU KNOW?**
>
> **This plot was foiled by a double agent!**
> Gilbert Clifford had agreed to work for Walsingham as part of his spy network. 'Agreed' is a loose term - he was threatened with death for him and his family if he didn't comply.

BABINGTON

The Babington Plot was a plot to assassinate Elizabeth and replace her with Mary, Queen of Scots. It was also used by Walsingham to entrap Mary and ensure her complicity in such plots could be proven.

What was the Babington Plot?

In the Babington Plot of 1586, plotters sought to kill Elizabeth, free Mary, Queen of Scots (p.45), and restore the Catholic faith in England. Letters between Mary and Babington were discovered by Elizabeth's spy network.

Who was involved in the Babington Plot?

The plot involved:
- Anthony Babington - a 25-year-old Catholic.
- John Ballard - a Jesuit priest.
- Mary, Queen of Scots (p.45).

Why did the Babington Plot fail?

The Babington plot failed for the following reasons:
- Babington openly expressed in a letter to Mary that Elizabeth must be killed.
- Mary, Queen of Scots (p.45), responded to Babington's letters agreeing to the plan.
- The letters were intercepted by Walsingham's spy network and decoded.

What were the consequences of the Babington Plot?
There were three main consequences of this plot.
- Mary was put on trial and eventually executed.
- Babington was tortured and executed.
- It led to retaliation against Catholics, with hundreds being arrested and some priests executed.

> **DID YOU KNOW?**
>
> **Babington and his men were young and naive, and it cost them!**
> When Mary responded to Babington and asked for the details of the plot, Walsingham took this as an opportunity to strike. He had one of his forgers copy Mary's handwriting and added an appendix asking for the names of all the plotters, to which they replied with a list of all involved!

COUNTER REFORMATION - CATHOLIC THREAT

The Counter-Reformation, also known as the Catholic Reformation, was the period of Catholic resurgence that happened in response to the Protestant Reformation.

What was the Counter-Reformation?
The Counter-Reformation was a movement in the Catholic church that tried to convert Protestants back to Catholicism. Missionaries were sent to England with the support of the pope.

Who were the Jesuits in the Counter-Reformation?
The Jesuits were important in the Counter-Reformation. They did not want direct rebellion but wanted to spread their religious message in England. Elizabeth saw them as a threat when they arrived in 1580.

Who was Edmund Campion in the Counter-Reformation?
In 1580 the Jesuits started their mission in England, led by Edmund Campion. Campion preached his message to ordinary English people all over the country but was eventually executed on suspicion of wanting to start a rebellion.

What was Elizabeth's response to the Counter-Reformation?
Elizabeth's tolerance, shown in the Religious Settlement *(p.43)*, faded later on in her reign as she became harsher in her treatment of Catholics.
- Recusancy fines were introduced for Catholics who did not participate in Protestant services. In 1581 this cost £20 - more than most people could afford.
- Any Catholic priests ordained after 1559 were viewed as traitors.
- The 1585 Act against Jesuits and seminary priests called for all Jesuits to be driven out of England.
- All English Jesuits were ordered to return to England and swear their loyalty to the queen, otherwise they faced execution for treason.

DID YOU KNOW?

It wasn't easy being Catholic in Elizabethan England!
Courts of inquiry extracted confessions by means of the rack or burning tongs. Jesuits were chased out of hiding, and even sometimes publicly disembowelled and dismembered!

PURITAN THREAT

The Puritans were members of a religious reform movement that arose within the Church of England in the late 16th century. They believed the Church of England was too similar to the Roman Catholic Church and should eliminate ceremonies and practices not rooted in the Bible.

What were Puritans?

Puritans were very extreme Protestants. They were unwilling to compromise over how they practised their faith and wanted to purify England of any Catholicism.

How did Puritans differ to moderate Protestants?

They wore simple, ordinary clothing and studied the Bible in detail. They rejected ceremony and held very simple services.

How did Elizabeth treat Puritans?

In the 1580s, Elizabeth took the same tough stance against Puritans as she did against Catholics. She appointed the anti-Puritan John Whitgift *(p.52)* as Archbishop of Canterbury.

Were there any powerful Puritans?

Parliament included a number of Puritans, including Robert Dudley and Sir Francis Walsingham.

Why were the Puritans a threat?

There are two reasons why Elizabeth saw Puritans as a threat.

- In the 1570s, Puritan prophesyings became popular. These meetings included members of the clergy and Elizabeth saw them as very dangerous.

- Puritans began to separate completely from the mainstream church. In 1580 they set up a new separatist church in Norwich. A second church was set up in London in 1592. However, the leaders of these churches were either arrested or hanged.

DID YOU KNOW?

They were big fans of education!
The Puritans believed in education and founded one of the most famous universities, Harvard, in 1636.

PRESBYTERIANS - PURITAN THREAT

Presbyterians were extreme Puritans, questioning the need for bishops and often criticising the queen and the Church.

What were Presbyterians?

Presbyterians were very extreme Puritans *(p.51)* who questioned the need for bishops at all. They often criticised the queen and the church during meetings called prophesyings (religious meetings).

> **DID YOU KNOW?**
>
> **They may not have made a impact during Elizabethan rule, but their time was coming!**
>
> Beginning in 1640, events occurred that moved Presbyterian Puritans towards the height of their power - a steady control of England by the Presbyterian parliamentary party.

RESPONSE TO THE PURITAN THREAT

John Whitgift was Elizabeth I's last Archbishop of Canterbury. He was suspicious of Puritans, and passionately defended the established Church.

Who was John Whitgift?

John Whitgift was the Archbishop of Canterbury from 1583 until his death in 1604.

What did John Whitgift think of Puritans?

Whitgift was anti-Puritan and was appointed by Elizabeth because she knew he would be harsh in his treatment of them.

What did John Whitgift do as Archbishop of Canterbury?

In 1583, Whitgift banned unlicensed preaching and enforced attendance at church through the introduction of recusancy fines.

> **DID YOU KNOW?**
>
> **John Whitgift liked to make an entrance!**
>
> He was known for his grand hospitality and had somewhat pretentious habits. A bit of a show off, he sometimes visited Canterbury and other towns attended by his advisers and up to 800 horses.

MARY QUEEN OF SCOTS' TRIAL

Mary's trial took place from 14th to 15th October, 1586, shortly after she was implicated in the Babington Plot.

What happened at the trial of Mary, Queen of Scots?

Mary, Queen of Scots *(p.45)*, was put on trial and executed because she was accused of being involved with a plot to assassinate Elizabeth I *(p.14)*.

Why was Mary, Queen of Scots, put on trial?

Mary was caught communicating with protagonists in the Babington Plot *(p.49)* of 1586, who planned to assassinate Elizabeth and put Mary on the English throne.

What was Mary, Queen of Scots' defence at her trial?

Mary argued her case strongly, claiming she could not be found guilty of treason because she was a foreign queen rather than an Englishwoman.

What punishment was Mary, Queen of Scots, given at her trial?

Mary was sentenced to death on 25th October, 1586.

Why did Elizabeth hesitate to sign Mary, Queen of Scots' death warrant after her trial?

There were two important reasons Elizabeth hesitated over signing Mary's death warrant.

- ☑ She was concerned it might lead to revenge attacks by Mary's son, King James VI of Scotland, or Philip II *(p.54)* of Spain.
- ☑ She was also concerned that if she legally killed a queen, it might undermine her own position and put her in danger later.

When was Mary, Queen of Scots, executed after her trial?

Mary was finally executed on 8th February 1587 at Fotheringhay Castle in Northamptonshire. Although Elizabeth had signed the death warrant, she had regrets about her decision.

What were the consequences of Mary, Queen of Scots' trial and execution?

These are the outcomes of Mary's execution:

- ☑ The result of Mary's execution was that there was no longer a Catholic alternative to Elizabeth as queen. However, many Catholics saw Mary as a martyr.
- ☑ The killing of Mary legitimised the idea of executing a queen and gave some of Elizabeth's less loyal subjects an idea.
- ☑ Scottish and French kings expressed their outrage at Mary's execution, although no action was taken.

DID YOU KNOW?

Mary wore red on her petticoat at her execution.

This colour wasn't a random choice, but the red of Catholic martyrdom. Mary was making a clear statement – she was anointed by God, to kill her was a sin, and in death she would become a holy martyr.

DETERIORATION IN RELATIONS WITH SPAIN

On top of religious tension between the Church of England and the rest of the Catholic world, England and Spain were rivals in the New World.

How can Anglo-Spanish relations during the reign of Elizabeth I best be described?

Throughout Elizabeth's reign *(p.16)* the relationship with Spain was strained. The relationship deteriorated over time and culminated in the attack of the Spanish Armada *(p.59)*.

What were Anglo-Spanish relations like under Mary I?

Before Elizabeth, England and Spain were united through the marriage *(p.19)* of Mary I and Philip II *(p.54)* of Spain from 1554 to Mary's death in 1558. England had even supported Spain in a war against France.

Why did Anglo-Spanish relations deteriorate under Elizabeth I?

There were many causes of the deterioration in relations:

- ☑ King Philip II *(p.54)* wanted to convert England back to Catholicism and therefore proposed to Elizabeth. She did not respond to his proposal.
- ☑ Elizabeth supported the Dutch rebels in their struggle against Spanish rule in the Netherlands as demonstrated in the Treaty of Nonsuch *(p.56)*, 1585.
- ☑ Robert Dudley became the Governor-General of the Netherlands, implying English control over the Spanish-controlled region.
- ☑ English privateers attacked Spanish ships and stole their treasure, the most notable being the raid on Cadiz in 1587.

DID YOU KNOW?

Spain was the most powerful country in the world!

Spain controlled a huge overseas territory in the New World, a big group of islands which they called 'the Indies' and territories in Europe, Africa and Australasia.

POOR RELATIONS WITH SPAIN - THE ROLE OF KING PHILIP II

Philip II of Spain was the ruler of one of the largest empires in history. A cautious reformer, he was also a devout Catholic during the Protestant Reformation. His religious piety often engaged him in conflicts with his neighbors that hurt his kingdom.

Who was King Philip II?

Philip II of Spain was married *(p.19)* to Elizabeth's sister, Mary I, making him the joint monarch of England. Their aim was to unite Catholic Spain and England. However, Mary's death in 1558, without children, prevented this.

How was Elizabeth's relationship with King Philip II?

Philip was angry when Elizabeth restored Protestantism as England's religion. He wanted control over England and proposed to Elizabeth, but she did not respond to his proposal.

How did Philip II behave towards Elizabeth I?

Philip II was loosely involved in the Ridolfi, Throckmorton, and Babington plots. However, he was keen to keep England as an ally and never did anything substantial, such as sending an army to invade, prior to 1588.

> **DID YOU KNOW?**
>
> **Philip II of Spain was a loner!**
>
> He had a palace, El Escorial, built in Spain and shut himself up there. Not far from Madrid, it was also close to the Sierra de Guadarrama, which was essentially a desert.

POOR RELATIONS WITH SPAIN - THE ROLE OF THE DUKE OF ANJOU

Francis, Duke of Anjou, was the youngest son of King Henry II of France. He was also a potential suitor for Elizabeth. He held protestant rebellions in the Netherlands and had hopes of becoming king there.

Who was the Duke of Anjou?

The Duke of Anjou was one of Elizabeth's suitors. He led Protestant rebels in the Netherlands against Spanish rule and wanted to become King of the Netherlands.

How did Elizabeth I support the duke of Anjou?

Elizabeth supported the Duke of Anjou and the Protestant rebels against Spanish rule in the Netherlands in a number of ways.

- ☑ She sent the Duke of Anjou £60,000 to support his ambition to become King of the Netherlands.
- ☑ In 1585, she signed the Treaty of Nonsuch *(p.56)*, giving the rebels even more support.
- ☑ She also sheltered some Dutch rebels, known as the sea beggars.

> **DID YOU KNOW?**
>
> **He was not always called Francis!**
>
> Francis was scarred by smallpox at the age of 8. It was felt this, along with his deformed spine, did not suit his birth name of Hercule. At his confirmation, his name was changed to Francis in honour of his late brother, Francis II of France.

POOR RELATIONS WITH SPAIN - THE ROLE OF THE NONSUCH TREATY

The Treaty of Nonsuch was a significant turning point for Elizabeth, confirming her support for the Dutch rebels. It was the final straw for Philip, who would then prepare the Armada.

What was the Treaty of Nonsuch?

The Treaty of Nonsuch was signed by Elizabeth I *(p.14)* and the Dutch rebels fighting against Spanish rule. It gave military support to the Dutch rebels and pledged England's protection.

> **DID YOU KNOW?**
>
> **Nonsuch Palace no longer exists!**
> Nonsuch Palace was demolished in 1583, so there is no such place anymore. See what we did there.....?

POOR RELATIONS WITH SPAIN - THE ROLE OF ROBERT DUDLEY

Robert Dudley, a favourite of Elizabeth I, was a Puritan, potential suitor and member of the Privy Council. He was also heavily involved in the Netherlands campaigns as Elizabeth sent him to command the English support forces during the Dutch revolt.

What was Robert Dudley's role in the Netherlands?

During the Protestant uprising against Spanish rule in the Netherlands, Dudley led 7,000 troops and became governor-general of the Netherlands.

Why was Dudley becoming Governor-General of the Netherlands a problem?

Dudley becoming Governor-General of the Netherlands implied that the English owned the Netherlands, thereby provoking King Philip II *(p.54)* as it was seen as an open act of war.

What was the outcome of Robert Dudley's involvement in the Netherlands?

The campaign was a mixed success, as although English troops did slow the advance of Spanish soldiers, it was an extremely campaign and Dudley fell out with his Dutch allies.

> **DID YOU KNOW?**
>
> **Dudley's actions in the Netherlands caused Elizabeth some anger.**
> He accepted the title of Governor-General in direct contradiction of her orders, and she insisted he resign.

POOR RELATIONS WITH SPAIN - THE ROLE OF THE ENGLISH PRIVATEERS

Privateering formed a key part of Elizabeth's naval strategy as she developed another naval force to help bring piracy under control. It was the privateers job to take or raid vessels belonging to an enemy government.

Who were the English privateers?

English privateers were private people or warships authorised by Elizabeth through the Lettres de Marque to attack foreign ships. This was very similar to how pirates operated.

What did the English privateers do?

Privateers would attack or capture treasure ships belonging to the enemy.

How was Elizabeth involved with the English privateers?

Privateers had to give a share of their loot to Elizabeth to gain legality for their actions. The amount of treasure she received from Sir Francis Drake, for instance, was huge.

> **DID YOU KNOW?**
>
> **English privateers also had a slightly different name!**
> They were also known as 'sea dogs'. Some of the most notably 'sea dogs' were Francis Drake and Walter Raleigh.

CADIZ - NAVAL WARFARE

Sir Francis Drake led a raid on the Armada at Cadiz in April 1587. This attack took the Spanish entirely by surprise, and Drake's manoeuvre set back the Spanish invasion by about a year.

What was the raid on Cadiz?

Sir Francis Drake and Robert Devereux raided Spanish Cadiz in 1587. They destroyed a total of 30 Spanish ships during this attack.

What was the raid of Cadiz known as?

The raid on Cadiz is known as Singeing the King of Spain's Beard.

What happened to the Armada following the Cadiz raid?

As a result of the raid, the ships being built for the Armada *(p.59)* were of a poorer quality and Spain's planned attack on England was delayed by a year.

> **DID YOU KNOW?**
>
> **On the way back from the raid Drake seized a passing ship, the Sao Felipe.**
>
> The contents on board were valued at £114,000 in 1587. That's roughly £20 million in today's money!

TACTICS AND TECHNOLOGY - NAVAL WARFARE

By the 1580s England had permanent dockyards and naval administrative institutions. It was able to send warships capable of fighting at sea to attack the Spanish in the Caribbean and in Spain itself, and able to confront the Spanish Armada with a formidable fleet.

What was the English Navy like under Elizabeth?

Henry VIII had created a fleet of fighting vessels to defend England, and its growth continued under Elizabeth. John Hawkins *(p.38)* was her naval commander.

What were the tactics of the English Navy during Elizabeth's reign?

They used three main tactics.

- ☑ A tactic called 'line of battle' where ships, in a single line formation, fired together on the enemy.
- ☑ Surprise raids were also a common tactic. The most famous was Drake's raid on Cadiz in 1587.
- ☑ 'Fireships' was a tactic where an old ship was set on fire and sent into the middle of the enemy, causing them to flee.

What new technology did the Elizabethan navy use?

There were two important advances in naval technology.

- ☑ The English had new lateen, or triangular, sails. These allowed for speed and agility, and more precise performance in battles and raids.
- ☑ More powerful cannons allowed more accurate fire at longer ranges.

What were the Spanish tactics used against the English Navy during Elizabeth's reign?

The Spanish tactic was to try and get close to enemy ships so their sailors could jump on board and attack them.

> **DID YOU KNOW?**
>
> **Elizabeth liked spending money on war and ships!**
>
> By 1588 the Exchequer was empty. Spending has risen from a pre-war average of £168,000 to £420,000 by 1588.

THE SPANISH ARMADA

The Spanish Armada was King Philip II's attempt at a seaborne invasion of England. It was the culmination of long-running rivalry between England and Spain over strategic, trade, and religious issues.

What was the Spanish Armada?
The Spanish Armada was a fleet of ships launched by Philip II *(p.54)* in an attempt to invade England.

When was the Spanish Armada attack?
The Spanish Armada attacked in 1588.

Who led the Spanish Armada?
The Armada was led by Alonso Perez de Guzman y de Zuniga-Sotomayor, the duke of Medina Sidonia.

What were the causes of the Spanish Armada?
There were five main causes for the attack by the Spanish Armada.

- The religious differences between the two countries were a main cause. Spain was Catholic while England was Protestant. The execution of Mary, Queen of Scots *(p.45)*, increased religious tensions as she was seen as a Catholic martyr by many.
- After Philip II *(p.54)* was widowed by the death of Mary I, he proposed to Elizabeth. His aim was to unite Spain and England under a Catholic king and queen. However, Elizabeth did not respond to his proposal.
- Elizabeth supported Protestant uprisings in the Spanish Netherlands in 1585, which angered Philip.
- Sir Francis Drake and other English privateers had spent years raiding Spanish ports and ships, and stealing treasures from Spanish colonies in South America. Elizabeth encouraged these acts.
- In 1570, Pope Pius V issued the papal bull that excommunicated Elizabeth from the Catholic church. This encouraged Philip II *(p.54)* to attack England.

What happened during the attack of the Spanish Armada?
There were four main events in the attack of the Spanish Armada in 1588.

- The Armada left Spain in May and reached Cornwall in July. The Armada was spotted off the coast and beacons were lit, sending news of their arrival. Philip was unprepared for a naval battle as he had filled his ships with land weapons, expecting hand-to-hand combat.
- On 6th August the Spanish fleet was anchored in Calais harbour, waiting for more soldiers from the duke of Parma. Drake sent in eight fireships, which caused the Armada to scatter and break its crescent formation.
- On 8th August at the Battle of Gravelines the English damaged many Spanish ships by firing from 100 metres away. The Spanish could barely defend themselves.
- Strong winds blew the Armada into the North Sea. They were forced to sail around Scotland and Ireland in order to return home. With no maps and bad weather, many ships were wrecked on rocks close to the shore or sank. Only 65 out of the 151 ships returned.

Why was the Spanish Armada defeated?
There were four main reasons for the defeat of the Armada.

- The weather blew the Armada into the North Sea, which were unsailed waters, causing many to sink.
- The duke of Medina Sidonia was an inexperienced sailor and an incompetent leader, whereas Francis Drake was an experienced sailor.
- The Spanish galleons were large and only used to the deep seas of the Mediterranean, not the shallower waters of the English Channel.
- The English had superior ships, weapons and tactics.

What were the main results of the defeat of the Spanish Armada?

There were four important results of the attack by the Spanish Armada.
- ☑ Elizabeth ransomed the captured Spanish troops and earned money to pay her navy *(p.58)* and nobles.
- ☑ King Philip II *(p.54)* planned two more attacks but one was unsuccessful and the other was never launched.
- ☑ The defeat of the Armada brought England together and strengthened the sense that England was living through a 'golden age *(p.24)*'.
- ☑ It proved that England was a major naval power.

> **DID YOU KNOW?**
>
> **The 'Little Ice Age' may have helped doom the Spanish fleet.**
> In 1558 there were unusually strong storms. As a result, the cold and stormy weather caused a significantly higher loss of life than direct combat.

THE ARMADA AND PROPAGANDA

The Armada Portrait is one of the most famous portraits in British history, showing an elegant and triumphant Elizabeth I after the defeat of the Spanish.

What was the Armada Portrait?

The Armada Portrait, from 1588, is thought to have been painted by George Gower. However, there is some uncertainty on this.

Why was the Armada Portrait considered propaganda?

The Armada Portrait can be considered propaganda for the following reasons:
- ☑ In the portrait, Elizabeth has her hand on a globe with her fingers on the Americas. This implies she has claim to the area owned by the Spanish.
- ☑ The left of the portrait shows the Armada *(p.59)* being destroyed by English fire ships, which is not what really happened.
- ☑ Elizabeth is wearing grand clothes, intended to make her look powerful.

> **DID YOU KNOW?**
>
> **The Tudors loved a copy and paste job!**
> There are actually three surviving Armada portraits! The overall design would have been approved, with artists then left to create their own copy of the design. These would have been given as gifts from the queen or acquired by those who wanted to show their affection and loyalty to Elizabeth.

GLOSSARY

A

Alliance - a union between groups or countries that benefits each member.

Allies - parties working together for a common objective, such as countries involved in a war. In both world wars, 'Allies' refers to those countries on the side of Great Britain.

Almshouse - charitable housing offering accommodation to poor people.

Ambassador - someone, often a diplomat, who represents their state, country or organisation in a different setting or place.

Apprenticeship - the arrangement whereby an untrained person is employed to learn a trade or skill.

Assassinate - to murder someone, usually an important figure, often for religious or political reasons.

Assassination - the act of murdering someone, usually an important person.

Astrolabe - an instrument that takes measurements of the sky and stars. Sailors devised hundreds of uses for it.

B

Bishop, Bishops - a senior member of the Christian Church, usually in charge of a diocese.

Bridewell - an early modern type of prison where vagabonds and prostitutes were whipped and made to work. They were also used to hold petty criminals awaiting trial.

C

Campaign - a political movement to get something changed; in military terms, it refers to a series of operations to achieve a goal.

Captive, Captivity - to be held in prison or confinement.

Catholic - a Christian who belongs to the Roman Catholic Church.

Circumnavigate - to travel around something or somewhere, commonly used to refer to sailing around the world.

Civilian - a non-military person.

Claim - someone's assertion of their right to something - for example, a claim to the throne.

Clergy - those ordained for religious duties, especially in the Christian Church.

Colonies, Colony - a country or area controlled by another country and occupied by settlers.

Colonisation - when one country encourages the migration of its people to another, with a view to bringing the second country under its control.

Colonists - people who settle in or inhabit another country, such as the British who went to America.

Commissions - the collective term for several organisations set up by the League of Nations to solve global issues.

Communal - referring to something that is shared by all members of a community, be it an action or possession etc.

Coronation - the ceremony of crowning a monarch.

Councillor, Councillors - a member of a council, often acting as an adviser to a monarch.

Credit - the ability to borrow money, or use goods or services, on the understanding that it will be paid for later.

Culture - the ideas, customs, and social behaviour of a particular people or society.

D

Daub - a way of making walls and buildings. The wattle, a woven lattice of wooden strips, is 'daubed' with a sticky substance made from a mixture of mud, clay, sand, animal dung and straw.

Debt - when something, usually money, is owed by a person, organisation or institution to another.

Decree - an official order with the force of law behind it.

Dispute - a disagreement or argument; often used to describe conflict between different countries.

Dissent, Dissenting - to hold or express views against an idea or policy, often in politics.

Dissolution, Dissolve - the formal ending of a partnership, organisation or official body.

E

Earl, Earls - the most important men in the country after the monarch during medieval times.

Economy - a country, state or region's position in terms of production and consumption of goods and services, and the supply of money.

Embassy - historically, a deputation sent by one ruler, state or country to another. More recently, it is also the accepted name for the official residence or offices of an ambassador.

Empire - a group of states or countries ruled over and controlled by a single monarch.

Enclosure - the process of dividing up large fields into privately owned, smaller pieces of land.

Excommunicate, Excommunication - to formally expel someone from the Catholic Church. Someone who is excommunicated is forbidden from participating in sacraments and services, and often believes their soul is condemned.

Extreme - furthest from the centre or any given point. If someone holds extreme views, they are not moderate and are considered radical.

F

Fasting - to deliberately refrain from eating, and often drinking, for a period of time.

Figurehead - Someone who acts as a symbolic leader for

GLOSSARY

something.

Foreign policy - a government's strategy for dealing with other nations.

G

Gentry - a high social class, coming below the nobility.

Golden Age - a phrase referring to a period of time considered prosperous, peaceful and happy, or when something was at its peak.

H

Harvest - the process of gathering and collecting crops.

Heir - someone who is entitled to property or rank following the current owner or holder's death.

Hierarchical - strongly organised into a hierarchy; ordering people according to how much power they have.

Hierarchies, Hierarchy - the ranking of people according to authority, for example a colonel in the army being higher than a corporal.

House of correction, Houses of correction - an early modern type of prison where vagabonds and prostitutes were whipped and made to work. They were also used to hold petty criminals awaiting trial.

I

Idle - to be lazy and avoid work, having no purpose and preferring to do nothing.

Illegitimate - the term given to a child born to unmarried parents; generally, not authorised by law.

Import - to bring goods or services into a different country to sell.

Independence, Independent - to be free of control, often meaning by another country, allowing the people of a nation the ability to govern themselves.

Industry - the part of the economy concerned with turning raw materials into into manufactured goods, for example making furniture from wood.

Inflation - the general increase in the prices of goods which means money does not buy as much as it used to.

Intellectuals - people with a high intellect who engage in critical thinking and reading, research, writing, and self-reflection about society.

K

Knighthood - the title, rank or status of a knight.

L

Labouring poor - those who owned no land and worked with their hands.

Lateen - a triangular sail on a long yard, mounted at an angle to the boat's mast.

Lease, Leases - a contract granting the use of something such as land or property for a specified period of time, usually in return for payment.

Legislation - a term for laws when they are considered collectively, for example housing legislation.

Legitimacy, Legitimate - accepted by law or conforming to the rules; can be defended as valid.

Literate - someone who can read and write.

Lord, Lords - a man of high status, wealth and authority.

M

MP - a member of parliament.

Martyr - someone who willingly dies for or is killed due to their beliefs, usually religious.

Mass - an act of worship in the Catholic Church.

Merchant, Merchants - someone who sells goods or services.

Middle class - refers to the socio-economic group which includes people who are educated and have professional jobs, such as teachers or lawyers.

Minister - a senior member of government, usually responsible for a particular area such as education or finance.

Monarchy - a form of government in which the head of state is a monarch, a king or queen.

Monasteries, Monastery - a religious building occupied by monks.

Monopolies, Monopoly - to control trade in a certain service.

Mullion, Mullioned - a glass window pane divided into small sections by vertical bars.

N

New World - the name given in the 16th century to describe the Americas and the Caribbean, distinguishing it from the 'Old World', which referred to Europe.

Nobility - the social class ranked directly below royalty.

Noble, Nobles - another word for aristocrat - a member of the highest and richest class in society.

O

Oath - a solemn promise with special significance, often relating to future behaviour or actions.

Ordained - to be made a priest or minister.

P

Papal bull - a public decree issued by the pope.

Parliament - a group of politicians who make the laws of their

GLOSSARY

country, usually elected by the population.

Patronage - the power to appoint people to certain positions and grant rights and privileges; can also refer to support given by a patron.

Pauper - a very poor person.

Persecute - to treat someone unfairly because of their race, religion or political beliefs.

Plague - a contagious disease that spreads rapidly.

Pope - the head of the Roman Catholic Church.

Population - the number of people who live in a specified place.

Poverty - the state of being extremely poor.

Preach, Preaching - to deliver a religious speech or sermon to a group of people.

Predecessor - the person who came before; the previous person to fill a role or position.

Prevent, Preventative, Preventive - steps taken to stop something from happening.

Printing press - a machine that reproduces writing and images by using ink on paper, making many identical copies.

Privateer, Privateers - a private individual who owned an armed boat and was authorised by the monarch to attack enemy treasure ships.

Propaganda - biased information aimed at persuading people to think a certain way.

Prophesyings - prayer meetings held by Puritans and Presbyterians.

Prosperity - the state of thriving, enjoying good fortune and/or social status.

Protestant - someone belonging to the branch of the Christian Church that separated from the Roman Catholic Church in the 16th century.

Provision - the act of providing or supplying something for someone.

Puritan - a Protestant Christian who followed very strict moral rules.

R

Radical, Radicalism - people who want complete or extensive change, usually politically or socially.

Raid - a quick surprise attack on the enemy.

Rebellion - armed resistance against a government or leader, or resistance to other authority or control.

Rebels - people who rise in opposition or armed resistance against an established government or leader.

Recusancy - the refusal to attend Protestant church services.

Reform, Reforming - change, usually in order to improve an institution or practice.

Reign - a period of power, usually by a monarch.

Relief - something that reduces pressure on people, often through financial or practical support.

Restoration - to return something to its former owner, place or condition; this includes returning a monarch to the throne or a head of state to government.

Royal prerogative - the term for the special rights, powers, and immunities to which the monarch alone is entitled under common law.

S

Secular - unconnected to religious or spiritual matters; not bound by religious rule.

Seminary priests - Roman Catholic priests who were trained in English seminaries or European study houses after laws were introduced forbidding Roman Catholicism in Britain.

Separatist - someone who supports a particular group of people or an organisation which is breaking away to work or live on their own.

Siege - action by enemy forces to surround a place or building, cutting off access and supplies, with the aim of either destroying it, gaining entry, or starving the inhabitants out.

Smallpox - a contagious and potentially fatal disease that causes a high fever, rashes and blisters.

State, States - an area of land or a territory ruled by one government.

Stately home - a large house, usually with an estate, owned by a rich, aristocratic family.

Strategy - a plan of action outlining how a goal will be achieved.

Submission, Submit - a formal surrender and acceptance of a new authority.

Succession - the process of inheriting a title, office or property.

Successor - someone who succeeds the previous person, such as a leader who takes over the role from the previous holder.

Suitor, Suitors - a potential marriage partner.

Superior - better or higher in rank, status or quality.

T

Tactic - a strategy or method of achieving a goal.

The crown, The throne - phrases used to represent royal power. For example, if someone 'seizes the throne' it means they have taken control. Can also refer to physical objects.

Treason - the crime of betraying one's country, often involving an attempt to overthrow the government or kill the monarch.

Treasury - a place or building where money or treasure is held; also refers to a government department related to finance and taxation.

Treaty - a formal agreement, signed and ratified by two or more parties.

GLOSSARY

V

Vagabond, Vagrancy, Vagrant - someone who wanders from place to place and has neither home nor job.

Voyage - a long journey involving travel by sea or in space.

W

Warrant - a document that allows something to happen legally, such as an arrest, search or administrative act.

Wattle, Wattle and daub - a way of making walls and buildings. The wattle, a woven lattice of wooden strips, is 'daubed' with a sticky substance made from a mixture of mud, clay, sand, animal dung and straw.

Welfare - wellbeing; often refers to money and services given to the poorest people.

Withdrawing chamber, Withdrawing room - a room used for entertaining in the 16th to early-18th centuries. It would now usually be called the living room.

Y

Yeoman - historically, a man who owned and cultivated his own farm.

INDEX

A
Age of Discovery - *40*
Anjou, Duke of - *55*
Architecture, Elizabethan - *27*
Armada - *59*
Armada Portrait - *60*

B
Babington, Anthony - *49*

C
Cadiz Raid - *57*
Counter-Reformation - *50*

D
Drake, Sir Francis - *37*
Dudley, Robert - *29*
Duke of Anjou - *55*
Dutch Revolt - *56*

E
Elizabeth I
    Challenges - *14*
    Early Life - *14*
    Government - *16*
    Marriage - *19*
    Navy - *58*
Elizabethan
    Education - *32*
    Exploration - *40*
    Government - *16*
    Leisure - *32*
    Navy - *58*
    Poor Laws - *36*
    Poverty - *33*
    Response to Poor - *35*
    Society - *23*
    Theatre - *25*
English Privateers - *57*
Essex Rebellion - *21*
Exploration - *40*

G
Globe Theatre - *26*

H
Golden Age - *24*

Hardwick Hall - *28*
Hawkins, John - *38*

K
Kenilworth Castle - *30*
King Philip II of Spain - *54*

M
Marriage - *19*

N
Navy - *58*
Netherlands
    Dudley - *56*
    Nonsuch - *56*
Nonsuch Treaty - *56*
Northern Revolt - *46*

P
Papal Bull 1570 - *47*
Paupers - *34*
Philip II, King of Spain - *54*
Plot
    Babington - *49*
    Northern Revolt - *46*
    Ridolfi - *48*
    Throckmorton - *48*
Poor Laws - *36*
Poverty - *33*
Presbyterians - *52*
Puritans - *51*

Q
Queen of Scots, Mary - *45*
    Trial - *53*

R
Raid of Cadiz - *57*
Raleigh, Sir Walter - *39*
Reformation
    Edward VI - *42*

INDEX

    Henry VIII - *41*

    Mary I - *43*

Relations with Spain - *54*

Religious Settlement - *43*

Response to Poor - *35*

Ridolfi, Roberto - *48*

S

Siege of Calais - *18*

Spanish

    Armada - *59*

    Raid of Cadiz - *57*

    Relations - *54*

Spanish Armada - *59*

T

Theatre - *25*

Throckmorton, Francis - *48*

Treaty

    of Cateau-Cambrésis - *19*

    of Nonsuch - *56*

W

Whitgift, John - *52*

Y

Years of Decline, Elizabeth I - *22*

www.ingramcontent.com/pod-product-compliance
Lightning Source LLC
Chambersburg PA
CBHW050718090526

44588CB00014B/2335